New Touchstones
11–14

Michael and Peter Benton

Hodder & Stoughton

A MEMBER OF THE HODDER HEADLINE GROUP

Orders: please contact Bookpoint Ltd, 130 Milton Park, Abingdon, Oxon OX14 4SB.
Telephone: (44) 01235 827720, Fax: (44) 01235 400454. Lines are open from 9.00–6.00,
Monday to Saturday, with a 24-hour message answering service.
You can also order through our website at www.hodderheadline.co.uk

British Library Cataloguing in Publication Data
A catalogue record for this title is available from The British Library

ISBN 0 340 68806 8
First published 1998
Impression number   10 9 8 7
Year   2004

Typeset by Multiplex Techniques Ltd, Kent.
Printed in Great Britain for Hodder & Stoughton Educational, a division of Hodder
Headline, 338 Euston Road, London NW1 3BH by J. W. Arrowsmith Ltd, Bristol

Contents

To The Teacher

The *Touchstones* anthologies have undergone several revisions since their beginnings in the 1960s, the last of which was just prior to the advent of the National Curriculum in the late 1980s. *New Touchstones* brings the anthologies up-to-date in a thorough-going reappraisal of the series in the light of the National Curriculum requirements at the different Key Stages. Just as Matthew Arnold's original idea of a 'touchstone' needs reinterpretation in successive generations, so the principles upon which the series is based, while remaining constant, simultaneously reflect the changing cultural conditions in which poetry teaching operates. These principles have proved both popular and durable. They are:

(i)   that an anthology of poetry for pupils should have a generous inclusiveness which acknowledges that the poems pupils may enjoy, feel provoked by, remember and, maybe, find valuable are as likely to come from a jokey performance script by Michael Rosen as they are from a sonnet by Shakespeare. Pupils should be offered a wide variety of voices; their poetry experience should neither be restricted by narrowness of vision nor limited to specifically targeted purposes. We abrogate our responsibilities as literature teachers if we allow the boundaries of poetry in school to be set solely by that which is officially examined.

(ii)   that a mix of old and new poetry is important. It is as misguided to think that what is 'relevant' to 1990s' pupils can only be poems written in the late twentieth century as it is to promote the study of pre-twentieth century poetry merely on the grounds of its 'heritage' status. Poems by Donne or Blake can have a good deal more relevance to life today than contemporary poems that foreground the ephemeral preoccupations of the present. Yet one of the advantages of poetry is its power to interpret the present for us. To set the work of recent writers in the context of that of their predecessors helps to illuminate the complementary qualities of both.

(iii)   that the concept of a 'teaching anthology' remains fundamental. The romantic notion that all teachers need to do is to read a lot of poetry to their classes so that its virtues, by some mysterious osmosis, will create a life-long love affair has long been discredited. Conversely, and far more apparent, there is the dislike that is generated in pupils by teachers who insist on line-by-line analysis which, in most cases, leads to the imposition of the teacher's views and the neglect of the pupils' responses. The approaches to teaching that we advocate are based on the premise that pupils' activities in reading and responding are the necessary preludes to their critical understanding of poetry.

(iv)　that 'creative' and 'critical' writing complement each other. Learning by doing is a natural process with poems. All pupils have something to say: by channelling their ideas and feelings into making their own poems as well as into commentary upon those of published poets, each informs the other. Pupils' criticisms gain the confidence of being written by 'practitioners' who have tried writing poems themselves; their imaginative writing gains from their developing knowledge of different forms and techniques.

New Touchstones has been composed with these principles in mind. It is constructed in three parts.

Part A: Ten Units

The purposes of this part of the book are to help pupils to enjoy and understand poems and to develop their knowledge of how they work. Each of the ten units aims to do three things:

(i)　to concentrate upon a main aspect of how poetry works, such as word sounds, imagery, or how feelings and ideas are expressed in different forms;

(ii)　to give one or more examples of these aspects at work in particular poems; and,

(iii)　to suggest ways in which pupils can talk and write about poetry and become more confident in expressing their views.

The units can be studied in any order. However, they have been sequenced to take pupils progressively from the relatively straightforward idea of pictures in words to the more sophisticated expression of feelings in poems. The units introduce some of the basic technical and figurative devices that poets use – metaphor, simile and personification; alliteration, assonance and onomatopoeia – as well as easily accessible forms such as haiku and ballads. None of these items can be separated out as neatly as this organisation into units suggests, but it is a convenient way of drawing attention to different aspects of how poems are written; it may also help to explain why some poems appeal to us more than others.

Where appropriate, we have included a brief list of poems elsewhere in the book which will take pupils further on the particular topic.

Part B: Ten Themes

Most poems are, by nature, 'solo performances' – responses to experience which stand on their own. Yet, similarities abound in subject matter, tone of voice, expressions of feelings and ideas, formal qualities and so on. While there will always be some sense of arbitrariness in thematic arrangements, nonetheless, it is clearly valuable to explore these similarities when they present themselves. The themes we have chosen are deliberately varied. Three are extensions of the units in Part A ('Word Pictures', 'Shapes and Sounds' and 'Ballads'). Some focus upon familiar surroundings and interpret aspects of home, family, sense of identity, school life and the natural world ('Me', 'School' and 'Seasons'); others, conversely, deal with the unfamiliar, the fantastic, or the nonsensical, where the rules of normal living are turned upside down ('Magic and Mystery' and 'Nonsense and Stuff'). There are also selections of poems under the headings of 'Stories' and 'Creatures' since these themes have a perennial appeal to this age group. The suggestions indicated by this icon for classroom activities at the end of each theme reflect both the autonomy of the individual poems and the advantages of comparative work. Talking, reading, writing, sketching, improvisation – all have a part to play in the study of poetry.

Part C: Ten Poets

The main criterion in this part of the book is to give a representative sample of each poet's work of sufficient substance for pupils to gain a clear sense of the writer's style, subject matter and way of looking at the world. The selection of poets was governed by the wish to include pre-twentieth century as well as contemporary writing and to indicate that poetry in English reflects a variety of cultural backgrounds. We did not want to duplicate material already published in our *Poetry Workshop* (1995) where, among others, James Berry and Grace Nichols were featured; but we have included one or two of their poems elsewhere in the book. We are aware that any list raises the question of exclusions as well as inclusions. It may be worth stating, therefore, that *for this particular age group* we formed a clear preference for Clare rather than Keats, for Tennyson rather than Browning, for Emily Dickinson rather than Emily Brontë. Often there are two or three poems by a pre-twentieth century writer that are suitable for 11–14 year olds, but our criterion of providing a sample of eight to ten poems has governed our choice of poets. Chaucer is featured here, too, as arguably the greatest storyteller in verse in English. We have included some support material in this section to help pupils overcome the initial oddities they may feel about the language and the culture. Here, as with the Introductions to all the ten poets, it is essential that the pupils are taken through the brief pen portraits in class and encouraged to ask questions and to find out more from the library and from the increasing number of audio and video resources available. Among the twentieth century poets, as in the rest of the book, there is a wide variety of single voices from a range of cultural backgrounds. We reject the distinction between 'our' and 'other' cultures, still evident in official curriculum documents, and the divisiveness it implies. The sheer variety of poetry in English is cause for celebration and sharing, not separateness. Poetry by John Agard or Maya Angelou *is a part of* an international literature in English, *not apart from* it. The pages entitled 'Ten Poets: Workshop' (pp. 217–220) give some additional information about the poets we have featured here and suggest several ways of exploring this material.

In the competition for time and attention in the National Curriculum, there is the danger that poetry is squeezed to the margins. When this neglect occurs pupils are short-changed; they are denied access both to that strand of literary history that has the longest and most distinguished pedigree and to an art form that has a peculiar ability to comment upon the culture and society in which they live. We hope that *New Touchstones* will encourage teachers and pupils to explore poetry widely, to enjoy the voices they encounter, and to gain a fuller knowledge of how poems work.

Michael and Peter Benton

PART A

Ten Units

Word-pictures

Making a picture with words is often not so easy as it looks at first. We all think that we can describe things clearly and vividly enough – after all, we are doing it in conversation every day – but as soon as we try to describe something in writing the right words slip out of place and will not make the picture we want from them. It's difficult to give the shape of the idea in our heads the same 'shape' in words. Here are three ways of making word-pictures.

(i) Snapshots

A camera can take instant pictures of people, scenes, animals, or anything that catches your eye. Your mind can take quick snapshots, too.

As a class

First, make sure paper and pencils are to hand. Then:

- close your eyes and concentrate on a single word – 'rat', 'stars', 'rocks' – it's best to chose the *name* of something that will set going lots of associations.
- when the picture in your mind's eye is clear enough, open your eyes and take your snapshot by jotting down as many words and phrases as you can to describe what you see. Do this quickly; don't worry about spelling or making sentences for the moment. The time exposure for your notes is only two minutes!

In pairs

After two minutes are up, talk about your jottings:

- Were there things you saw in your mind's eye that you couldn't find words for?
- Can you and your partner add any words or phrases to each other's notes?

On your own

- Now, compose your picture. Arrange your notes, adding new words and crossing out ones you don't want, and try to make a two- or three-line snapshot. When the words are as you want them, write out a fair copy, checking your spelling and punctuation so that your picture is as clear as possible. (You could present each poem on a separate postcard to make a wall display.)

(ii) Haiku

There is one sort of poem that is as brief and precise as these snapshots: it is called haiku and originally comes from Japan. As you will see from the following examples, haiku poems are only three lines long and, because of their shortness, they cannot include a lot of detail. Haiku poets have to choose their words carefully because they are using so few. The poems may suggest a scene or incident, they may create an atmosphere, they may express a person's feelings, or they may do several of these things at the same time.

Here are two haiku poems which create pictures:

FULL MOON

Bright the full moon shines:
on the matting of the floor,
shadows of the pines.

KIKAKU

SUMMER NIGHT

A lightning flash:
between the forest trees
I have seen water.

SHIKI

As you see, these are clear, simple word-pictures in which the writer concentrates on one central object or scene and leaves the reader to imagine the details of the landscape.

In pairs

● What other details of the picture do you see in your 'mind's eye' when you read each of these poems? Describe the scene in each poem in your own words and see what details you add.

These haiku poems focus on two specific scenes. The first one does not explain which room the full moon is shining into, what sort of matting is on the floor, or what shape the shadows are; nor does the second one tell us what sort of lightning flashed or whether a lake or river or the sea has been glimpsed through the trees. Instead, each poem *shows* us an instant snapshot, like the one you have made.

If you want to take better photographs you cannot just point your camera and hope for the best. In the same way, if you want to make better word-pictures, snapshots are a start but soon you have to think a bit about composition. This is easy with haiku because the poems do not have to rhyme (even though some translated ones, like 'Full Moon', may rhyme the first and third lines). The basic form is a seventeen-syllable poem, the syllables being arranged 5, 7, 5 over three lines.

Here is a regular haiku written by someone of school age.

RAIN HAIKU

Gentle summer rain;	(5)
Scratch, scratch upon the window	(7)
With its little stick.	(5)

COLIN ROWBOTHAM

On your own

Once you feel confident with your snapshots, try to write a regular haiku in this pattern. With a little practice you should find that you can come fairly close to the 5, 7, 5 pattern. First, be sure you understand what a syllable is. (The easiest way is to check out a few first names in your class: John is one syllable, Susan is two, Christopher is three. . .). Then, either redraft your 'snapshot' as a haiku or invent a new one.

In pairs or groups

Try writing a haiku sequence of, say, four poems for the seasons of the year, or twelve poems to make a haiku yearbook in which you catch the picture of January, February, March and so on. Or, read through the following poems and then see if you can add one or two other examples of 'housework haiku'.

HOUSEWORK HAIKU

I
The mirror is blurred.
I polish till it reflects
A room undisturbed.

II
The washing machine
Is conditioned to begin
Its neurotic spin.

III
Handwashing cotton
Connects me with the women
Time has forgotten.

IV
Instead of tea leaves,
Clairvoyants could have a laugh
With hairs in the bath.

V
The bin liner bursts,
Vomiting ever thicker
Cold chicken tikka.

VI
I am hypnotized
Ironing at massage speed
Yet another sleeve.

VII
The growling Hoover
Is very hungry to feed.
It strains on its lead.

VIII
I shall take a poll
To see how many people
Replace the loo roll.

SARAH WARDLE

(iii)   Thumbnail sketches

In these short, sketch-like haiku poems, the reader has to fill out the picture by thinking round the few words that are given. Here is another word-picture (not a haiku this time) which suggests a good deal more than it actually states.

IN A STATION OF THE METRO

The apparition of these faces in the crowd;
Petals on a wet, black bough.

EZRA POUND

This poem was arrived at after a lot of hard work on a much longer version of the same idea. The poet's job was to prune away unnecessary words so that this finished poem would represent, in this sharp, uncluttered way, the experience of seeing a crowd of people in an underground station.

As a class

- What is the connection between the first line and the second?
- Why does the poet use the word 'apparition'?

On your own

- Try to write a few lines which capture vividly and precisely any scene that sticks in your mind: it might be a sunset or a power-station. Whatever you choose, when you have a first draft of, say, five or six lines, try cutting away the unnecessary lines or phrases until you have two or three lines which say just what you want.

Further Poems

Metaphors and Similes

(i) Two sorts of comparison

When we want to tell other people about things we have seen or done, or feelings we have had, we often use comparisons. We see a likeness between two things and decide to focus on that and for the time being forget any differences. Here are two haiku poems which use comparisons.

IN THE MOONLIGHT

It looks like a man,
the scarecrow in the moonlit night –
and it is pitiful.

SHIKI

THE BARLEYFIELD

Up the barley rows,
stitching, stitching them together,
a butterfly goes.

SORA

The first poem makes a direct comparison: the scarecrow is like a man. The second poem *assumes* the comparison of the bobbing movement of the butterfly to be similar to the movement of someone stitching.

You may know these two types of comparison already as *simile* and *metaphor*. Both can make poems vivid and more exciting. They help poets to say more exactly what they mean, and they make both the poet and the reader use their imagination.

You can see how appropriate it is to describe poems like these, which are similar to sketches or drawings, as 'word-pictures'. In fact the haiku writer is doing in words what the artist is doing in the picture opposite, which is also Japanese in origin. Look at the details of the picture carefully.

As a class

- What is the object behind the raised prow in the background of the picture – a mountain or another wave?
- What does the falling spray remind you of?
- What does the foaming crest of the wave look like?

In answering these questions you will find that you have to try to think of comparisons.

On your own

- Now write a haiku of your own about this great wave in which you make use of one of these comparisons.

(ii) Look again

Comparisons help us to look at things in a fresh and original way. Writers often put two things together which we would not normally connect. D H Lawrence, for example, describes bats flying in the evening air as 'bits of umbrella'. Gareth Owen begins a poem about a waterfall like this:

'When the river threw itself off the cliff
It spun a twist of rope
So as not to lose touch with itself.'

Ted Hughes describes planet Earth in its orbit –

'With arms swinging, a tremendous skater
On the flimsy ice of space,
The earth leans into its curve –'

All these comparisons allow us to see the thing being described more clearly.

On your own

Read through the following twelve comparisons. They are all extracts from longer poems, apart from 'May Poem' which is complete. As you read, give the words time to form a picture in your mind. Make some jottings to help you remember this picture. Then ask yourself:

- Which comparisons did you like?
- Which ones did you not see at all?
- Select your favourite extract and write a sentence saying what you like about the comparison.

(1) PIGEONS

Small blue busybodies
Strutting like fat gentlemen
With hands clasped
Under their swallowtail coats

RICHARD KELL

(3) SUNFLOWERS

Three astonished sunflowers
topping the garden wall.
frilled faces saucer-eyed
at being there.
giraffe-tall, gormless somehow,
heads hanging
over the next garden.

PHOEBE HESKETH

(2) THE IMPRINT OF A SEA-SHELL ON A STONE

And chiselled clear on stone
A spider-web of shell,
The thumb-print of the sea.

NORMAN NICHOLSON

(4) A BUTTERFLY'S WINGS

On silent hinges
open-folds her wings
applauding hands.

MAY SWENSON

(5) A DONKEY

His face is what I like.
And his head, much too big for his body — a toy head,
A great, rabbit-eared, pantomime head,
And his friendly rabbit face,
His big, friendly, humorous eyes — which can turn wicked,
Long and devilish, when he lays his ears back.

But mostly he's comical — and that's what I like.
I like the joke he seems
Always just about to tell me. And the laugh,
The rusty, pump-house engine that cranks up laughter
From some long-ago, far-off laughter-less desert —

The dry, hideous guffaw
That makes his great teeth nearly fall out.

TED HUGHES

(6) MAY POEM

rain falls

the candy-floss tree
rains confetti and
bridesmaids

pink snowdrifts
lie on the path

GERDA MAYER

(7) SNOWFLAKES

Snowflakes
like tiny
insects
drifting
down.

JOHN AGARD

(8) BOREDOM

Boredom
Is
Clouds
Black as old slate
Chucking rain straight
On our Housing Estate
All grey
Day long.

GARETH OWEN

(9) WORKMEN RETILING A ROOF

there are men
on the roof of the church,
playing patience,

tile after tile,

CRAIG RAINE

(10) A DOCKER

There, in the corner, staring at his drink.
The cap juts like a gantry's crossbeam,
Cowling plated forehead and sledgehead jaw.
Speech is clamped in the lips' vice.

SEAMUS HEANEY

(11) FOG

The yellow fog that rubs its back upon the window-panes,
The yellow smoke that rubs its muzzle on the window-panes
Licked its tongue into the corners of the evening,
Lingered upon the pools that stand in drains,
Let fall upon its back the soot that falls from chimneys,
Slipped by the terrace, made a sudden leap,
And seeing that it was a soft October night,
Curled once about the house, and fell asleep.

T S Eliot

(12) A PINEAPPLE

The hut stands by itself beneath the palms.
Out of their bottle the green genii come.
A vine has climbed the other side of the wall.
The sea is spouting upward out of rocks....

The lozenges are nailed-up lattices.
The owl sits humped. It has a hundred eyes.
The cocoanut and cockerel in one.

Wallace Stevens

In groups

Choose your own subject, one that you could describe in several ways (an eye, electricity pylons, the London Underground, a tower block, say) and each of you make up one line or phrase, using a comparison if possible, to describe it. Sort out the best order for your lines, think of a title, and write out your group poem.

Further Poems

Ted Hughes:	'Spring Nature Notes'	p. 126
	'Work and Play'	p. 128
	'October Dawn'	p. 205
Anna Adams:	'Warning to a Worm'	p. 120
Richard Kell:	'Pigeons'	p. 121
Alfred, Lord Tennyson:	'The Eagle'	p. 168
Phoebe Hesketh:	'Kingfisher'	p. 190
	'Cats'	p. 191

Word-pictures and Ideas

(i) Pictures into ideas

How do you write a poem about a rainbow without mentioning any of its colours? Like this! Hear the poem read aloud.

RAINBOW

When you see
de rainbow
you know
God know
wha he doing —
one big smile
across the sky —
I tell you
God got style
the man got style

When you see
raincloud pass
and de rainbow
make a show
I tell you
is God going
limbo
the man doing
limbo

But sometimes
you know
when I see
de rainbow
so full of glow
and curving
like she bearing child
I does want know
if God
ain't a woman

If that is so
the woman got style
man she got style

JOHN AGARD

As a class

- Rehearse one or two 'readings' of the poem, perhaps sharing the sections between several readers. The language and the rhythm of the lines mean that you need to give your performance the sound of West Indian English. Try to get the feel of the Caribbean as you speak the lines aloud. (See pp. 210–216 for other poems by John Agard.)
- What do you make of the unusual idea in the third section?

(ii) Ideas into pictures

One technique often used by poets, particularly when they want to express an abstract idea, is that of 'personification'. You will see what this means from these two word-pictures. They were written 400 years ago by Edmund Spenser (c. 1552–1599). Here is his picture of Despair. It's a gloomy portrait to begin with; by the end it is a gory one. Hear the description read aloud, either to the whole class or within a group.

That darkesome cave they enter, where they find
   That cursed man, low sitting on the ground,
   Musing full sadly in his sullen mind;
   His greasy locks, long growen, and unbound,
   Disordered hung about his shoulders round,
   And hid his face; through which his hollow eyne★   ★eyes
   Looked deadly dull, and stared as astound;
   His raw-bone cheeks through penury and pine,
Were shrunk into his jaws, as he did never dine.

His garment nought but many ragged clouts,
   With thorns together pinned and patched was,
   The which his naked sides he wrapped about;
   And him beside there lay upon the grass
   A dreary corpse, whose life away did pass,
   And wallowed in his own yet lukewarm blood,
   That from his wound still welled fresh alas;
   In which a rusty knife fast fixed stood,
And made an open passage for the gushing flood.

And here is Gluttony. Again, hear the poem read aloud.

And by his side rode loathsome *Gluttony*,
   Deformed creature, on a filthy swine,
   His belly was up-blow with luxury,
   And eke with fatness swollen were his eyne,
   And like a crane his neck was long and fine.
   With which he swallowed up excessive feast,
   For want whereof poor people oft did pine,
   And all the way, most like a brutish beast,
He spewed up his gorge, that all did him deteast.

In green vine leaves he was right fitly clad;
   For other clothes he could not wear for heat,
   And on his head an ivy garland had,
   From under which fast trickled down the sweat;
   Still as he rode, he somewhat still did eat,
   And in his hand did bear a boozing can,
   Of which he supped so oft, that on his seat
   His drunken corpse he scarce upholden can,
In shape and life more like a monster, than a man.

In pairs

Talk about the pictures of these two characters that you get in your mind's eye. Then see if you can illustrate these descriptions, perhaps with a poster poem on which you include a few lines as a part of the picture.

Writing about ideas as if they were people is not as difficult as it might seem at first. Some ideas are already associated with well-known personifications – Time as an old man with a scythe; New Year as a baby; or Love as either a mischievous Cupid or a sensuous Venus. Talk about how you might personify these ideas and others such as Hate, Envy, Anger, Fear, Spring, Winter . . . Is the figure to be male or female? Young or old? What does it look like? What is its mood? List your ideas and then work on *one* of them to make a short description. If you choose Winter then Arcimboldo's painting below may help you with the details.

(iii) Ways of seeing

The next poem is about seeing the invisible! First, read it through to yourself and you will see that it is a series of word-pictures of things that the wind does and does not do. Then in pairs, read it aloud, taking alternate verses.

WORKINGS OF THE WIND

Wind doesn't always topple trees
and shake houses to pieces.

>Wind plays
>all over woods, with weighty ghosts
>in swings in thousands,
>swinging from every branch.

Wind doesn't always rattle windows
and push, push at walls.

>Wind whistles
>down cul-de-sacs and worries
>dry leaves and old newspapers to leap
>and curl like kite tails.

Wind doesn't always dry out
sweaty shirts and blouses.

>Wind scatters
>pollen dust of flowers, washes
>people's and animals' faces
>and combs out birds' feathers.

Wind doesn't always whip up waves
into white horses.

>Wind shakes up
>tree-shadows to dance on rivers,
>to jig about on grass, and hanging
>lantern light to play signalman.

Wind doesn't always run wild
kicking tinny dustbin lids.

>Wind makes
>leafy limbs bow to red roses
>and bob up and down outside windows
>and makes desk papers fly up indoors.

JAMES BERRY

In pairs

Talk about what you see in your mind's eye from these ten pictures of the workings of the wind. Here are two ways of working on the poem:

● Copy out the poem carefully down the left-hand side of a sheet of plain paper and draw a series of framed miniature pictures alongside to illustrate each verse. Keep your drawings simple; perhaps concentrate on just a single detail each time.
● Can you and your partner add a pair of verses to the poem, describing other things the wind does and does not do?

James Berry gives us his picture gallery of the effects of the wind. Ted Hughes gives us a gale force blast: notice in the following poem how all the comparisons help to create this one idea. Hear the poem read aloud.

WIND

This house has been far out at sea all night,
The woods crashing through darkness, the booming
  hills,
Winds stampeding the fields under the window
Floundering black astride and blinding wet

Till day rose; then under an orange sky
The hills had new places, and wind wielded
Blade-light, luminous black and emerald,
Flexing like the lens of a mad eye.

At noon I scaled along the house-side as far as
The coal-house door. Once I looked up –
Through the brunt wind that dented the balls of my eyes
The tent of the hills drummed and strained its guyrope,

The fields quivering, the skyline a grimace,
At any second to bang and vanish with a flap:
The wind flung a magpie away and a black-
Back gull bent like an iron bar slowly. The house

Rang like some fine green goblet in the note
That any second would shatter it. Now deep
n chairs, in front of the great fire, we grip
Our hearts and cannot entertain book, thought,

Or each other. We watch the fire blazing,
And feel the roots of the house move, but sit on,
Seeing the window tremble to come in,
Hearing the stones cry out under the horizons.

TED HUGHES

On your own

- Either, write out the text of the poem on a separate sheet, or use a photocopy. Spend five minutes re-reading the poem and making your own jottings *around* the poem about the phrases you like, words you don't understand, the feelings the description gives you, the pictures you get in your mind's eye and so on. Your notes might look something like this.

house like a ship in a storm

This house has been far out at sea all night

lots of active verbs suggest gale-force winds { *The woods crashing through darkness, the booming hills* } *sounds*

Winds stampeding the fields under the window

Floundering black astride and blinding wet

These are two or three things we noticed about the first verse. Continue with your own notes for the rest of the poem.

In groups

- Find out what each of you has noticed about the poem. In particular, which comparisons seemed most vivid? One of them may suggest an idea for an illustration to accompany a phrase or line from the poem; or, as a group, you could divide up the verses and work on a picture sequence for the whole text. Notice how the poem moves from darkness to dawn, to noon, to afternoon, and finishes, it seems, in front of the evening fire.

On your own

- Look back at your own notes on the poem. Choose the phrases which you think best express the idea of the wind. Write a 'Wind Haiku' using your own and Ted Hughes' words.

Further Poems

Po Chu-i:	'The Red Cockatoo'	p. 56
Philip Larkin:	'Tops'	p. 56
Max Endicoff:	'The Excavation'	p. 58
William Langland:	'The Covetous Man'	p. 58
John Clare:	'An Idle Hour'	p. 164
Phoebe Hesketh:	'Clown'	p. 189

Ballads

(i) Ballads of all sorts

What are they?   You will know that a ballad is a popular song that tells a story. Ballads have a long history; they are very different from the tiny, tightly packed haiku poems which we looked at earlier. They sometimes tell their stories at great length. Several of the old Robin Hood ballads have more than 90 verses! These stories in verse were very popular with all sorts of people and many of them survive today as folk songs. Ballads have always had a strong connection with music. The early ballads were composed not as poems to be read but as songs to be sung or danced or even worked to.

How were they made?   Although there were professional ballad makers and singers, the author of a ballad might be almost anyone – a farmer, an innkeeper, a shepherd, a tinker, a travelling pedlar – and he was probably not an author as we use the word for he would not write his story down. He would remember it and perhaps change the story very slightly each time he told it. New verses would be added, unsuccessful verses would drop out. People who heard the song would perhaps remember parts of it and add their own words to fill in the gaps. They might even add bits from a ballad they already knew and so a different version would be born.

What are they about?   Ballads were about many things – tales of adventure; religion; magic; daily life. In mediaeval England there were still many who had a strong belief in magic, and women were frequently executed for practising witchcraft. Alongside the Christian religion the old pagan beliefs still flourished, particularly in the country areas, and many ballads reflect these beliefs. 'The Unquiet Grave' (p. 71) for example is a religious poem but has a ghostly theme. A few ballads on Christian subjects have been preserved into the present day as carols. 'The Cherry-tree Carol' on p. 72 and 'Mother and Maiden' on p. 72 are two of the best.

Work songs   People who work at repetitive tasks often sing to pass the time and to take their minds off the monotony of the job. This is as true today as it was in mediaeval England where such tasks as spinning and weaving, grinding and mowing, ploughing the fields and rocking the cradle were all part of the daily routine. An example of this kind of ballad is one which you may well know from when you were younger – *One Man Went to Mow*. Apart from these there are those ballad songs composed and sung by sailors to help them keep time in tasks such as hauling up the anchor and setting the sails.

● What is the special name given to sailors' work songs?

Sensational stories   About 400 years ago a new kind of ballad developed. Booksellers and printers realised that these poems were very popular and soon ballads were printed and sold by the thousands in both town and country. Travelling pedlars and street ballad mongers made their living by them and, to sell more copies, they concentrated on crime, violence and scandal. For example, as late as 1849 the ballad of Rush's murder sold 2,500,000 copies.

● What was the new development that put such ballad mongers out of business?

Ballads today   Nowadays ballads are everywhere – from the pop charts to poetry books, from TV commercials to church services. Folk songs, work songs and carols continue to be written and sung; and poets continue to write ballad poems. One of these is Charles Causley and two of his ballads are on pp. 23 and 75. Changes in popular music this century have affected the ballad more than anything else. Whether you are interested in rock, modern folk songs, country and western or another sort of music, you will probably be able to find variations of the ballad. Look at the words of one or two recent songs.

● Are they the same as or different from the lyrics of the more traditional ballads?

(ii) Performing a ballad

The ballad of Sir Patrick Spens supposedly tells a story about the king of Scotland being persuaded to send Sir Patrick on a dangerous sea journey in bad weather to bring back the daughter of the king of Norway in 1285. Little more is known about the real events, and, as the ballad was printed five hundred years after they were supposed to have happened, it may all be fiction.

As a class

● Hear the poem read over once to get the story clear in your mind.

SIR PATRICK SPENS

The king sits in Dunfermline town
    Drinking the blood-red wine:
'O where will I get a good sailor,
    To sail this ship of mine?'

Up and spake an elder knight,
    Sat at the king's right knee:
'Sir Patrick Spens is the best sailor
    That ever sailed the sea.'

The king has written a braid* letter   *long
    And sealed it with his hand.
And sent it to Sir Patrick Spens
    Was walking on the strand.

'To Noroway, to Noroway,
    To Noroway o'er the foam;
The king's own daughter of Noroway,
    'Tis thou must bring her home!'

The first line that Sir Patrick read
    A loud, loud laugh laughed he:
The next line that Sir Patrick read
    The tear blinded his ee.*   *eye

'O who is this has done this deed,
    This ill deed unto me;
To send me out this time o' the year
    To sail upon the sea?

'Make haste, make haste, my merry men all,
    Our good ship sails the morn.'
'O say not so, my master dear,
    For I fear a deadly storm.

'I saw the new moon late yestere'en
    With the old moon in her arm;
And if we go to sea, master,
    I fear we'll come to harm.'

They had not sailed a league, a league,
   A league, but barely three,
When the sky grew dark, the wind blew loud,
   And angry grew the sea.

The anchor broke, the topmast split,
   'Twas such a deadly storm.
The waves came over the broken ship
   Till all her sides were torn.

O long, long may the ladies sit
   With their fans into their hand
Or ere they see Sir Patrick Spens
   Come sailing to the strand.

O long, long may the maidens stand
   With their gold combs in their hair,
Before they'll see their own dear loves
   Come home to greet them there.

O forty miles off Aberdeen
   'Tis fifty fathom deep.
And there lies good Sir Patrick Spens
   With the Scots lords at his feet.

ANON

● Discuss any points you find you are not sure about. Notice how we are simply given an outline, not a lot of detail. What description there is helps the story along; the emphasis is upon the action. Notice, too, how the story develops in a series of 'flashes', rather like a film cutting from one event to another.

Vss 1 + 2		Vs 3		Vss 4–6		Vss 7 + 8
Dunfermline		The King		*Aberdeen*		Spens gives
The King asks	→	writes and	→	Spens receives	→	instructions
for a good		seals the letter		the letter as he		to prepare to
sailor to bring		to Spens.		walks along		leave for
his daughter				the coast.		Norway.
home from						
Norway.						

	Vss 9 + 10		Vss 11 + 12		Vs 13
	North Sea		The sailors'		*North Sea*
	The ship is hit	→	wives wait in	→	The ship sinks
	by a storm and		vain for the		with all hands
	breaks up.		ship's return.		40 miles off
					Aberdeen.

In groups

- Prepare a group performance of the ballad. Think carefully about who is speaking and what their feelings are likely to be. There are several different ways of splitting up the verses between different readers but you might find it useful to think of having the following five voices:
  — a narrator who reads the opening two lines and picks up the story whenever no other character is speaking.
  — a king (who speaks only two lines in the first verse)
  — the 'elder knight' in verse two
  — Sir Patrick Spens
  — A sailor in verses 7 and 8 who begins 'O say not so'

The last three verses are all very similar in style and mourn the death of Sir Patrick and the sailors. They can each be read by a different voice rather than the narrator if you choose. This would mean using eight voices rather than five. When you are satisfied with your version, perform it for the rest of the class and/or tape record it.

(iii) Making a ballad

Here are a few simple guidelines and an example to help you to write your own ballad. It is probably best to work in pairs.

- Agree on a story. Battles, disasters, ghosts are all common in older ballads, as we have seen. Traditional stories make good topics – the creation of the world in seven days, or Noah's ark, or Christmas or other festivals; but you can choose a more modern subject, as in the 'fight ballad' below, such as a football match, a race, a school trip with lots of incidents, or the bare bones of a story or play you have read, or a soap opera story.
- Work out a story-plan for about six verses, perhaps set out like the one above. Keep it simple. Make sure your story has a beginning, middle and end.
- Read through several ballads and listen particularly to the rhythms and rhymes. A common pattern is to have a four-line verse in which lines 1 and 3 are longer than the others and where lines 2 and 4 rhyme.
- Decided on the pattern that sounds best to you and write your first verse. If you get stuck, don't worry; leave a gap and try a later verse on your story-plan.
- When you finish your ballad, write out a fair copy and illustrate it boldly so that it can be put up on display.

Here is an example of a modern ballad written by a boy of thirteen. We have altered two or three lines slightly, just to smooth out the rhythm; otherwise, it's all his own work.

THE BALLAD OF BOVVER PETE

In a house
On Windblown Street,
Lived a boy
Called bovver Pete.

He wore big boots
Upon his feet,
A real tough nut
Was bovver Pete.

He'd go out all day
Walking tall,
And practise bovver
On a hard brick wall.

His head was hard
As hard as brick,
He was very tough
But also thick.

Yes bovver Pete
Man he was tough,
But he met his match
In Jim Macduff.

Now bovver Pete
He picked a fight,
With Jim Macduff
One winter's night.

Now bovver Pete
He gave him nuts,
And quickly followed
With a few head-butts.

Now Jim got angry
Took out his blade,
And Pete now became
Just second-grade.

Now Pete he slowly
Backed away,
He wanted to live
Till another day.

But Jim struck quick
His knife felt blood,
And Pete did fall
In the filthy mud.

Now bovver Pete
He's gone up top,
To the skinhead club
And the bovver shop.

Now everyone will remember Pete,
And take off their hats and say:
He wasn't really all that bad
In his own sorta way.

EFSTATHIOS

(iv) Mystery story

The poem 'What has Happened to Lulu?' is a modern story written in ballad form.

As a class

Hear the poem read aloud.

WHAT HAS HAPPENED TO LULU?

What has happened to Lulu, mother?
   What has happened to Lu?
There's nothing in her bed but an old rag doll
   And by its side a shoe.

Why is her window wide, mother,
   The curtain flapping free,
And only a circle on the dusty shelf
   Where her money-box used to be?

Why do you turn your head, mother,
   And why do the tear-drops fall?
And why do you crumple that note on the fire
   And say it is nothing at all?

I woke to voices late last night,
   I heard an engine roar.
Why do you tell me the things I heard
   Were a dream and nothing more?

I heard somebody cry, mother,
   In anger or in pain,
But now I ask you why, mother,
   You say it was a gust of rain.

Why do you wander about as though
   You don't know what to do?
What has happened to Lulu, mother?
   What has happened to Lu?

CHARLES CAUSLEY

In pairs

- Decide what you think has happened to Lulu.
- Discuss what you imagine is the state of mind of the three characters – the younger child who asks the questions, the mother, the missing Lulu. What evidence do you have? Share your ideas with the rest of the class then hear the poem read again.

Further Poems

Anon: 'The Twa Corbies'   p. 70
Charles Causley: 'The Ballad of Charlotte Dymond' p. 75
Anon: 'The Cherry-tree Carol'   p. 72
S T Coleridge: 'The Rime of the Ancient Mariner' p. 81
Alfred, Lord Tennyson: 'Lady Clare'   p. 170

UNIT 5

Patterns on the Page

In pairs

- Flick through the pages of this book and jot down the titles of poems that make different shapes on the page. Can you find:
  — short, chunky poems that sit square on the page with no separate verses
  — long, thin poems that go from top to bottom of the page (and sometimes onto the next one)
  — poems in neat, four line, rhymed verses
  — poems that sprawl and have lines of very different lengths
  — neat little two line poems
  — poems that are arranged in a design or picture?
- Try to find examples of each of these, jotting down the page numbers. Note down examples of any other shapes you find. Talk about why you think the writers have chosen these particular shapes for these particular poems.

Writers deliberately choose the line length, the pattern on the page, the overall shape of the poem that best suits their purpose. The look of the poem on the page is not an accident. In a way the poem's shape signals what sort of poem it is likely to be as well as saying to us 'this is a poem'.

(i) Traditional ballad form

As a class

- Hear these three opening verses of different poems read aloud and decide what sort of poem might follow:

The king sits in Dunfermline town
  Drinking the blood-red wine:
'O where will I get a good sailor,
  To sail this ship of mine?'

★★★

Mary stood in the kitchen
   Baking a loaf of bread.
An angel flew through the window.
   'We've a job for you,' he said.

★★★

It is an ancient Mariner,
And he stoppeth one of three,
'By thy long grey beard and glittering eye,
Now wherefore stopp'st thou me?'

- How do you know that these are not just four line poems each complete in itself but that something must follow?

The simple form of the verses on the page, their regular rhymes and rhythms invite us to settle back and listen to a good story. They are all examples of the traditional *ballad* form of verse and a ballad tells a story. You will find more on ballads on pp. 70–77.

(ii) Free verse

The next poem also tells a story. D H Lawrence was watching swallows flying in the gathering gloom of evening beneath the arches of the Ponte Vecchio bridge in Italy. He suddenly realised that he was not watching swallows any longer but that bats had taken their place.

As a class

- Hear these lines from the poem read aloud and think about what effect the line lengths and the spaces on the page have on the way it is read.

Like a glove, a black glove thrown up at the light
And falling back

Never swallows!
Bats!
The swallows are gone.

At a wavering instant the swallows give way to bats
By the Ponte Vecchio . . .
Changing guard

- What is different about its shape on the page from the shape of the three ballad verses you looked at before?
- Why do you think the poet chose this way of setting his poem out on the page?
- What is the effect of the one word *Bats!* being put on a line by itself?
- Why do you think the poet leaves two blank lines instead of running the lines together with no spaces?

This sort of writing is called *free verse*. You will find other examples of free verse like this on pp. 184 and 186. Remember free verse doesn't mean the writer chops up the lines into uneven lengths just for the sake of it: there's usually a reason.

(iii) Picture Poems

In pairs

Look at the way another poet, George Macbeth, wrote about touching his cat, Peter:

You can touch
his
feet, only
if
he is relaxed.
He
doesn't like it.

He could have written this: 'You can touch his feet only if he is relaxed. He doesn't like it.'

- Why do you think the poet set the lines out like this on the page? (Think of a sleeping cat, totally relaxed. How does it help us to 'see' the cat in our mind's eye?)
- How does laying out the lines like this suggest we might say them? (Think about how it might help us to feel the cat's response to the light touch of fingers on its four paws).

Sometimes writers arrange their poems so that the words actually make an outline picture or a recognisable shape on the page, which helps us see and experience more clearly what is being described. Writers often enjoy playing with words in this way and we hope you will too.

On the next page is 'The Mouse's Tail' from Lewis Carroll's *Alice's Adventures in Wonderland*.

In threes

- Work out a reading of the poem with one of you reading the narrator's lines, another reading Fury's speech starting at 'Let us both go to law' and a third reading the mouse's lines. Are you going to get louder or softer towards the end? faster or slower? nicer or nastier? You decide and then perform your versions for the class.

'Mine is a long and a sad tale,' said the Mouse, turning to Alice,
and sighing.
'It *is* a long tail, certainly,' said Alice, looking down with wonder
at the Mouse's tail; 'but why do you call it sad?' And she kept on
puzzling about it while the mouse was speaking so that her idea of
the tale was something like this:

"Fury said to
a mouse, That
he met in the
house, 'Let
us both go
to law: *I*
will prose-
cute *you*. —
Come. I'll
take no de-
nial: We
must have
the trial:
For really
this morn-
ing I've
nothing
to do.'
Said the
mouse to
the cur.
'Such a
trial, dear
sir. With
no jury
or judge
would
be wast-
ing our
breath.'
'I'll be
judge.
I'll be
jury,'
said
cun-
ning
old
Fury:
'I'll
try
the
whole
cause,
and
con-
demn
you to
death.'"

A boy wrote about the first time his pet cat saw snow like this:

AMAZED CAT

You can even shape a poem around the positions of a football team if you like! This one by Roger McGough takes some careful reading to sort out at first but it does make sense (and it rhymes!).

In pairs

● Work out the words of the two verses and each practise saying one of them. When you think you can do it, show the rest of the group.

CUP-FINAL

T. O'Day

W. E. March　　　T. O. G. Lory

J. Usty　　　O. Uwait.　　　N. See

G. O'Dow

A. Day　　　W. Ewill　　　N. Inf.a.　　　H. I. Story

Young　　　N. Fast　　　M. O'Reskill　　　I. T. Sreally

W. Egot

A. L. L. Sewnup　　　W. E. Rethel　　　A. D. S. Whollrun

A. Round　　　W. Embley

W. I. Thecup

ROGER MCGOUGH

One picture poem which has survived for over two hundred years was inscribed by a glazier (a man who cuts and fits the glass into windows) on a window in the Plumbers' Arms, in York. In 1789 he took his diamond cutting tool and inscribed this poem on the glass in the shape of a cut diamond.

A GLAZIER'S VERSE

```
                          A
                       glazer  I
                  Am      and      I
                  work     for     my
              bred      and      many
          fine     window    in    my
          time     have    I     made
      I    with    my    dimond    have
      Cut    out    the    Glass    and
          in   a   Corner   Cist   many
                a  prity  lass  1789
```

In pairs

● The glazier's spelling was a little different from modern spelling. Can you find the five words which he spells differently from the way we would today?
● The glazier chose a diamond because that is what he worked with. Think about other jobs with which we might associate a shape. Share your ideas with the rest of the group.

On your own

● Try writing a poem of your own designed to fit a shape. You could invent one that matches a particular job. Perhaps a hammer or a saw for a builder; an open goal for a footballer; a triangle or a cone for a roadworks man . . . whatever you think appropriate. You could start with the same phrase as the glazier but change it: 'A - - - am I'.
Or, if you prefer, you could just try a shape: a triangle or circle. Or you could try the shape of something like a rocket, a church, an eye, a parachute, a snail, a fish, a snake. Don't forget the words and the shape should help each other.

Further Poems

E. E. Cummings:	'one/this/snowflake . . .'	p. 63
Grace Nichols:	'Snowflake'	p. 62
E. E. Cummings:	'in Just-spring'	p. 127
Edwin Morgan:	'Spaceman 3: Off Course'	p. 64
Edwin Morgan :	'The Computer's First Christmas Card'	p. 65
D H Lawrence:	'Bat'	p. 184

Sounds

In pairs

- SLITHY … MIMSY … UFFISH … Three words you may not have come across before. Say them over to yourself a few times: try them out. In pairs, decide what they might mean and quickly jot down any ideas they may suggest or anything they may describe. Share your ideas with the rest of the class.

As a class

- Hear Lewis Carroll's nonsense poem 'Jabberwocky' read aloud. As you read it or hear it read, listen to the strange sounds and see the pictures they conjure up in your mind's eye.

JABBERWOCKY

'Twas brillig, and the slithy toves
   Did gyre and gimble in the wabe:
All mimsy were the borogoves,
   And the mome raths outgrabe.

'Beware the Jabberwock, my son!
   The jaws that bite, the claws that catch!
Beware the Jubjub bird, and shun
   The frumious Bandersnatch!'

He took his vorpal sword in hand:
   Long time the manxome foe he sought—
So rested he by the Tumtum tree,
   And stood awhile in thought.

And as in uffish thought he stood,
   The Jabberwock, with eyes of flame,
Came whiffling through the tulgey wood,
   And burbled as it came!

One, two! One, two! And through and through
   The vorpal blade went snicker-snack!
He left it dead, and with its head
   He went galumphing back.

'And hast thou slain the Jabberwock?
  Come to my arms, my beamish boy!
O frabjous day! Callooh! Callay!'
  He chortled in his joy.

'Twas brillig, and the slithy toves
  Did gyre and gimble in the wabe;
All mimsy were the borogoves,
  And the mome raths outgrabe.

LEWIS CARROLL (1832–1898)

Lewis Carroll loved making up words like 'tulgey', 'frabjous' and 'borogoves'. In Chapter Six of *Through the Looking Glass*, which is where the poem first appeared, Humpty Dumpty explains to Alice the meaning of some of the words:

' "*Brillig*" ', he says, 'means four o'clock in the afternoon – the time when you begin *broiling* things for dinner' and ' "slithy"' means "lithe and slimy" . . . there are two meanings packed up into one word.'

- Of course, his explanations are not the only possible ones. Did 'brillig' and 'slithy' suggest something different to you?

On your own

- So far you have tried to explain three of the words; now, on your own, jot down the ideas suggested to you by some of the others:

toves	gyre and gimble
mome raths	borogoves
frumious	outgrabe
manxome	vorpal
galumphing	beamish

In pairs

- Compare your ideas about the meanings of the words. How far do you agree? Are there certain similarities?

In groups

- Work out a dramatic reading of the poem that you can perform for others and/or tape record. There are many possible ways of approaching it. For example, you could work in groups of about six and read the first and last verses as a group with two other voices reading the two parts in inverted commas and a narrator reading the middle three verses. Experiment! Add weird and wonderful sound effects if you like.

If you are really adventurous you could add these two French and German translations of the first verse! Amazingly, they sound quite convincing.

Il brilgue: les toves lubricilleux
Se gyrent en vrillant dans le guave.
Enmimés sont les gougebosqueux
Et le momerade horsgrave.

(French)

Es brillig war. Die schlichten Toven
Wirrten und wimmelten in Waben;
Und aller-mumsige Burggoven
Die mohmen Rath' ausgraben.

(German)

On your own

● Experiment with writing your own nonsense verse. Be careful not to use too many nonsense words: Lewis Carroll uses many more normal words and phrases than he does invented ones. You could write a sequel to 'Jabberwocky'. Look at the second verse again: the Jabberwock is only one of three possible attackers the hero has to face. Write your own poem about the meeting of a hero or heroine with either the Jubjub bird or the frumious Bandersnatch.

In groups

● Read this description of somebody washing up a sticky porridge pan. It comes from a longer poem called 'Sink Song'.

Scouring out the porridge pot,
    Round and round and round!

Out with all the scraith and scoopery,
Lift the eely ooly droopery,
Chase the glubbery slubbery
    gloopery
    Round and round and round!

(FROM Sink Song, J A LINDON)

There are several invented words here but if you have ever washed up a porridge pan you will know how well they describe the rubbery skin and the slimy strings of porridge sticking to its sides and the sucking, slopping sounds of the 'glubbery slubbery gloopery'. And if you have never done the washing up, reading this gives you a good idea of what it is like. The sounds suggest feelings.
Here the writer chooses words to sound like the thing he is describing. There is a special word for this effect – it is called *onomatopoeia*. It's a long word for something very ordinary: we all of us use onomatopoeia when we use words like 'cuckoo', 'babble', 'boom', 'slurp', 'squelch'.

● Make a list in your groups of as many words whose sound suggests their meaning, *onomatopoeic words*, as you can think of.

On your own

● Listen to these two words, say them aloud to yourself:
Malooma . . . . Taketi . . . . Malooma . . . . Taketi
Now jot down which of these shapes is the Malooma and which is the Taketi:

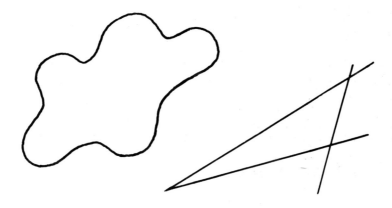

As a class

● Do you agree or disagree which is which? Why do you think people chose as they did?

In pairs

● Here are a dozen words. Sort them into two lists – one for 'Maloomas' and one for 'Taketis':

balloon	icicle	snatch	vicious
mushroom	oozing	picnic	lash
tripping	summer	puddle	volume

● Compare your lists with those of others.
● How did you decide which words to put in each list?
● Did you find some words more difficult to classify than others?
● Why do you think this was?

Your two lists of words are useful to show you how some words may suggest different qualities by their sounds and their associations: these may not only be 'malooma' qualities of roundness or bulkiness or 'taketi' qualities of sharpness and quickness, but also such things as warmth or coldness, lightness or heaviness.

In pairs

- Do the same kind of list-making for the following lines:

(1) AN ICICLE:

Feel the chilling spear
Sending shivers through my hand
Cold and glacial knife.

(2) A SUMMER EVENING:

The velvet hum of evening

(3) BLADES OF GRASS:

Only some spires of bright green grass,
Transparently in sunshine quivering.

(4) BODIES FALLING LIFELESS:

With heavy thump, a lifeless lump,
They dropped down one by one.

(5) THE SOUND OF BEES:

And murmuring of innumerable bees

(6) FISHERMEN GUTTING FISH AT THE DOCKS:

    . . . the clockwork men

Incise and scoop the oily pouches, flip
The soft guts overboard. . .

    . . . the slapping silver turns
To polished icy marble upon the deck.

- Did you agree or disagree which list each should be in?
- Did any seem to be a mixture?

Further Poems

Sounds and Movement

In pairs

- Read over these lines from a poem describing a cat which has slipped out of the house and into a warm greenhouse:

slipping impossibly in,
flattening my fur at the hush and touch of the sudden warm air,
avoiding the tiled gutter of slow green water,
skirting the potted nests of tetchy cactuses . . .

- Copy out the lines leaving a space between each line.
- Now put a ring around any sounds which are repeated close to each other. You could start on line 1 by ringing the 's' in 'slipping' and the 'ss' in 'impossibly' and then there are the 'p' sounds in both words. Oh, and the 'l' sounds . . . You might even ring the 'in' sound and the word 'in' at the end of the line.
- Try doing the same thing with the rest of the lines yourself.
- You will find lots of repetitions of the same sounds. Read the lines aloud once again. Why do you think the writer chose the sounds he did in each case? What is the effect of the repeated 'c', 'k' and 't' sounds and all the short vowel sounds in the last line? What is the contrasting effect of the long, open vowel sounds in a phrase like 'slow green water'?

As a class

- Share your ideas and see if you can all agree on which sounds are repeated and what the effects are. It's useful to collect all your ideas on the board.

As you will have noticed when you said the lines aloud, the sounds the poet has chosen affect the movement of the verse, slowing us down and speeding us up in such a way that we create the mood he wants. He can make us slow and sleepy or sharp and prickly simply by choosing the right sounds. This writer also controls the way we read the lines by placing words describing the cat's movement at the beginning of each line: 'slipping', 'flattening', 'avoiding', 'skirting' and their linked sounds suggest the sleek movement of the cat.

Sound and movement help to create the pictures in our mind's eye. The technique of repeating certain consonants for such effects is known as *alliteration*. When vowels (a, e, i, o, u) are repeated for similar effect it is called *assonance*. The first world war poet, Wilfred Owen once wrote the line:

Only the stuttering rifles' rapid rattle

to suggest the hard, mechanical sound and rapid movement of a fusillade of shots.

On your own

- Say the line out loud to hear yourself imitating a short burst of rifle fire.
- Copy out the line; put a ring round the repeated consonants and underline the vowels.

In pairs

- Read the following lines aloud and discuss how their sound and movement echo their sense and help us to see the images in the mind's eye.

(1) PIGEONS COOING TO THEMSELVES:

Only the warm dark dimples of sound
Slide like slow bubbles
From their contented throats.

(2) A SNAKE DRINKING FROM A WATER-TROUGH:

He drank enough
And lifted his head, dreamily, as one who has drunken,
And flickered his tongue like a forked night on the air, so black,
Seeming to lick his lips . . .

(3) CHILDREN SKATING ON A LAKE AND SHOUTING TO EACH OTHER:

So through the darkness and the cold we flew,
And not a voice was idle: with the din
Smitten, the precipices rang aloud;
The leafless trees and every icy crag
Tinkled like iron.

(4) AN OLD WOLF:

Lopes on purpose, paddling the snow
Of the soft-blown winterlocked landscape,
Under the loaded branches in the hush of forests.

(5) A CLAMOROUS PEAL OF CHURCH BELLS:

The five old bells
Are hurrying and stridently calling,
Insisting, protesting
They are right, yet clamorously falling
Into gabbling confusion, without resting
Like spattering shouts of an orator endlessly dropping
From the tower on the town, but endlessly, never stopping.

In groups

The next poem is a dog's-eye view of a cat chase that should leave you breathless.

● Prepare a reading of the poem which captures all the sound, energy and movement of the chase. You might find it helps to have a group of two or three to speak the longer lines in chorus and to use single voices for the dog and cat noises.

CAT

Cat!
  Scat!
atter her, atter her,
Sleeky flatterer,
Spitfire chatterer,
Scatter her, scatter her
  Off her mat!
  Wuff!
  Wuff!
  Treat her rough!
Git her, git her,
Whiskery spitter!
Catch her, catch her,
Green-eyed scratcher!
  Slathery
  Slithery
  Hisser,
  Don't miss her!

Run till you're dithery,
  Hithery
  Thithery!
  Pfitts! pfitts!
How she spits!
  Spitch! spatch!
  Can't she scratch!
Scritching the bark
Of the sycamore-tree,
She's reached her ark
And's hissing at me
  Pfitts! pfitts!
  Wuff! Wuff!
Scat,
Cat!
That's
That!

ELEANOR FARJEON

The idea of alliteration is as old as poetry itself and in fact most early poetry in English was full of alliteration. The poem below about the blacksmiths dates from a very early period in our literature. Its robust use of alliteration works brilliantly to conjure up the smithy of centuries ago.

In groups

● After hearing the poem read aloud once and clearing up any problems, prepare your own reading of it. Split the lines up between you and enjoy the texture and the sound of this alliterative verse.

THE BLACKSMITHS

Swart, swarthy smiths besmattered with smoke
Drive me to death with the din of their dints.
Such noise on nights heard no one never;
What knavish cry and clattering of knocks!
The snub-nosed changelings cry after 'Coal! Coal!'
And blow their bellows till all their brains burst:
'Huff, puff!' pants one; 'Haff, paff!' another.
The spit and sprawl and spin many yarns;
They grind teeth and gnash them, and groan together,
Hot with the heaving of their hard hammers.
Aprons they have of hide of the bull.
Their shanks are shielded from the fierce sparks:
Heavy hammers they have, that are hard handled;
Stark strokes they strike on an anvil of steel.
Lus, bus! Las, das! they strike in rotation:
The Devil destroy such a doleful din.
The master lengthens a little piece, belabours a
    smaller,
Twines the two together, and strikes a treble note
Tik, tak! Hic, hac! Tiket, taket! Tik, tak!
Lus, bus!, Las, das! such lives they lead
All horseshoers; Christ give them sorrow
For none of these water burners at night may rest

ANON

Further Poems

Sound, Movement and Rhythm

Rhythm in poetry is a kind of pattern which underlies and holds together the whole structure. Sometimes, as in music, the rhythm may be so strong that it is the most important part of the poem; sometimes it is deliberately played down and is quiet and unnoticed – but it is almost always there.

In groups

This poem by the Caribbean poet, John Agard, captures the mechanical movement and the sound of a woodpecker rhythmically tapping a tree trunk.

● Decide how you are going to split the poem up. There are lots of possibilities. You may like to consider having voices quietly repeating the second verse throughout the reading as a background; you may even split the lines so that each line is said by a different voice. Or you may think of a quite different way. Keeping time can be tricky: you will probably find that the rhythm of the poem makes you break up words into two syllables so that, for example 'carving' becomes 'car/ving'.

WOODPECKER

Carving
tap/tap
music
out of
tap/tap
tree trunk
keep me

busy
whole day
tap/tap
long

tap/tap
pecker
birdsong
tap/tap
pecker
birdsong

tree bark
is tap/tap
drumskin
fo me beak
I keep
tap/tap
rhythm
fo forest
heartbeat

tap/tap
chisel beak
long
tap/tap
honey leak
song
pecker/tap
tapper/peck
pecker
birdsong

JOHN AGARD

In another poem about a woodpecker, Ted Hughes makes quite a different use of rhythm. Rhyme is important here too.

As a class

- Hear the poem read aloud.
- What gives the verses their jaunty repeated rhythm? (You may find it helps to count the syllables in each line and to tap out the rhythm of the verse as you say it. Can you see a pattern?).

WOODPECKER

Woodpecker is rubber-necked
  But has a nose of steel.
He bangs his head against the wall
  And cannot even feel.

When Woodpecker's jack-hammer head
  Starts up its dreadful din
Knocking the dead bough double dead
  How do his eyes stay in?

Pity the poor dead oak that cries
  In terrors and in pains.
But pity more Woodpecker's eyes
  And bouncing rubber brains.

TED HUGHES

A quite different kind of rhythm underlies Edward Brathwaite's poem 'Limbo'. In a limbo dance the dancer sways backwards closer and closer to the ground and almost parallel to it so as to pass under a very low bar. It is a tourist attraction these days in the Caribbean where Brathwaite comes from but the dance dates back to the days of slavery. The only way that the wretched chained slave could exercise in the dark, stinking holds of the old slave ships was by moving in this cramped fashion.

● Hear the poem read aloud.

In groups

● Prepare a dramatised reading of the poem, calling up different voices in turn. Try to let the haunting limbo rhythm which is almost like a spell, speak through the poem.

LIMBO

And limbo stick is the silence in front of me
limbo

limbo
limbo like me
limbo
limbo like me

long dark night is the silence in front of me
limbo
limbo like me

stick hit sound
and the ship like it ready

stick hit sound
and the dark still steady

limbo
limbo like me

long dark deck and the water surrounding me
long dark deck and the silence is over me

limbo
limbo like me

stick is the whip
and the dark deck is slavery

stick is the whip
and the dark deck is slavery

limbo
limbo like me

drum stick knock
and the darkness is over me

knees spread wide
and the water is hiding me

limbo
limbo like me

knees spread wide
and the dark ground is under me

down
down
down

and the drummer is calling me
limbo
limbo like me

sun coming up
and the drummers are raising me

out of the dark
and the dumb gods are raising me

up
up
up

and the music is saving me

hot
slow
step

on the burning ground.

EDWARD KAMAU BRATHWAITE

W H Auden's poem 'The Quarry' which tells of someone betrayed to
the soldiers by a lover is powerful largely because of its insistent
rhythm and repetitions which build up to the climax of the last verse.
The drumming of the soldiers which opens the poem is kept in our
minds as the story unfolds. The word 'quarry' in the title means
someone who is hunted down as prey, a victim.

In pairs

● Read the poem together. The person being hunted asks the questions in
each verse and the lover gives the answers.

As a class

● Listen to different readings of the poem. Talk about the images that the
poem leaves in your mind and what makes them so strong.

THE QUARRY

O what is that sound which so thrills the ear
  Down in the valley drumming, drumming?
Only the scarlet soldiers, dear,
  The soldiers coming.

O what is that light I see flashing so clear
  Over the distance brightly, brightly?
Only the sun on their weapons, dear,
  As they step lightly.

O what are they doing with all that gear,
  What are they doing this morning, this morning?
Only their usual manoeuvres, dear,
  Or perhaps a warning.

O why have they left the road down there,
  Why are they suddenly wheeling, wheeling?
Perhaps a change in their orders, dear,
  Why are you kneeling?

O haven't they stopped for the doctor's care,
  Haven't they reined their horses, their horses?
Why they are none of them wounded, dear,
  None of these forces.

O is it the parson they want, with white hair,
  Is it the parson, is it, is it?
No, they are passing his gateway, dear,
  Without a visit.

O it must be the farmer who lives so near.
  It must be the farmer so cunning, so cunning?
They have passed the farmyard already, dear,
  And now they are running.

O where are you going? Stay with me here!
  Were the vows you swore deceiving, deceiving?
No, I promised to love you, dear,
  But I must be leaving.

O it's broken the lock and splintered the door,
  O it's the gate where they're turning, turning
Their boots are heavy on the floor
  And their eyes are burning.

W H Auden

Although reading aloud and performing poems is often suggested in this book, the next poem is actually written as a *performance poem*, which means it was written specifically to be performed to an audience. The two authors and performers are Ian McMillan and Martyn Wiley who form the duo, Yakety Yak. The story of Derek, a rather sad young man in an anorak who spends all his time spotting trains, needs all the drive and energy you can give it!

In groups

- Read the poem through once to feel the rhythms and the movement of the lines. Notice how they often imitate the rhythmic sound of a train as in the first four lines. Notice too how certain sections build up the tension through rhythmic repetition as in the sections beginning 'Derek's ready' and how they end in a climax and then an anti-climax 'WHOOSH!' followed by 'MISSED IT!'
- Agree how you will divide the lines between the different voices in the group: some will be individual lines with single voices; some will be spoken as a group; some will be soft, others loud; some will build to a climax. Sometimes there may be a dramatic pause in the action. You decide and then practise your reading to perform to the rest of the class or to record on tape. You could dramatise the piece with a 'Derek' character being watched by the speakers and you could add appropriate sound effects if you wanted.

TRAINSPOTTER

Trainspotter trainspotter trainspotter
Train train
Trainspotter trainspotter trainspotter
Train train

He's got the anorak
He's got the duffle bag
He's got the big notebook
And a pocket full of pens
Fountain pens and cartridge pens
And all those flippin' biros

And all those flippin' biros
Derek's ready
Derek's ready
Derek's ready

For the
Red light
Orange light
Green light
GO!
WHOOSH!
MISSED IT!

Trainspotter trainspotter trainspotter
Train train
Trainspotter trainspotter trainspotter
Train train

He's got the thermos flask
He's got the sandwiches
He's got the big bag of crisps

And a pocket full of sweets
Chocolate bars and Yorkie bars
And all those flippin' Penguins
And all those flippin' Penguins

Derek's ready
Derek's ready
Derek's ready
For the
Red light
Orange light
Green light
GO!
WHOOSH!
MISSED IT!

Missed it. Again.

Have another go
Have another go
Get a closer look
Get a closer look
At the
Red light
Orange light
Green light
GO!
WHOOSH!

Ouch!!
Caught it!!
Right in the back
Right in the back
Right in the back of the anorak.

So now they're spotting Derek
So now they're spotting Derek

Trainspotter trainspotter trainspotter
Train train
Trainspotter trainspotter trainspotter
Train train

They've got the duffle bag
That's in Crewe
They've got the family bag of crisps
That's in Wick
They've got the big notebook
That's loose leaf –
Covers all the regions

Covers all the regions
Mind you so does Derek
Mind you so does Derek
With his
Red light
Orange light
Green light
GO!
WHOOSH!!

Trainspotter trainspotter trainspotter
Train train
Trainspotter trainspotter trainspotter
Train train
Neeeyaah!!

YAKETY YAK

Further Poems

Five Senses

Sight, Hearing, Touch, Smell, Taste. . . We rely on our five senses to tell us what's going on.

As a class

● Close your eyes for a minute and, without talking to anybody else or touching them, concentrate on what you can hear, touch, smell and taste. Now open your eyes and quickly jot down what you noticed.

You can probably *hear* the shuffle of feet, creak and scrape of furniture, whispers and half-stifled giggles around you. Concentrate and try to remember which sounds were close to you (could you hear your own heart?). Which sounds were near? What could you hear in the middle distance? Could you pick up anything from far off?

What could you tell by *touching* things? You may have noticed the cold, hard shape of your pencil, the sharp edge of a piece of paper, the texture of your clothes. . . anything else?

And, resisting the temptation to be rude about your friends, what about *smell*? Polish, leather, plastic, wool, rubber, even cooking smells from the kitchens may all have been noticeable. . . anything else?

Taste probably tells you least of all but there may be something . . . If there is, then jot it down.

● Share your notes with the rest of the class, perhaps by making four lists on the board.
● Now, hear the following two poems read aloud. Both are about 'the sounds of silence': the first about some imaginary sounds in the natural world; the second about tiny sounds sensed within a quiet room.

LISTEN

Silence is when you can hear things.
Listen:
The breathing of bees,
A moth's footfall,
Or the mist easing its way
Across the field,
The light shifting at dawn
Or the stars clicking into place
At evening.

JOHN COTTON

QUIET

The night was so quiet
That the hum of the candle burning
Came to my ear,
A sound of breath drawn through a reed
Far off.

The night was so quiet
That the air in the room
Poised, waiting to crack
Like a straining
Stick.

The night was so quiet
That the blood and the flesh,
My visible self sunk in the chair,
Was a power-house giant, pulsing
Through the night.

RICHARD CHURCH

On your own

- Use one of these poems as a model to turn your notes into a poem of your own. The first one invites you to write a list poem beginning 'Silence is when you can hear things. Listen: . . .' – then, list the things you heard around you in the classroom. If you use the second, your poem might begin, 'The room was so quiet / That. . .'.

Writers often concentrate hard on what their senses tell them, hoping to recreate the same sort of experience for their reader. This poem is by a writer who is putting off writing: instead he sharpens his pencil. Hear the poem read aloud.

SHARPENER

The sharpener peels a conical fan,
A paint-trimmed petticoat of scented curls
Tickles my knuckles, rasps spiralling down
And graphite dully shines in finger whorls.

I tap the cold, hard cylinder against my teeth,
Admire its smooth and perfect taper,
Taste damp wood and thin, anaemic lead beneath,
Reluctantly commit myself to paper.

PETER BENTON

As a class

- Sight is obviously very important in the poem, but what other senses are brought into play?
- Different rooms around school have their own atmospheres. Perhaps you remember going into a science laboratory for the first time.
  — What were your first impressions as you entered?
  — What sights, sounds and smells hit your senses?
  — Can you find words for the taste of some smells?
  — Do you remember. . . bottles of chemicals arranged in racks? . . . the cones of flame on the bunsen burners?. . . tall stools and long benches? . . . tripods, flasks and strangely shaped glassware?
- Jot down your ideas quickly and then use them as the basis for a poem which tries to capture the sense of the place as it appeared to you.
- Of course you may prefer to choose some other place you know well. What sense impressions would you jot down if you were trying to capture the feeling of being in a gym? on the side of a swimming pool? in the dining hall? in the IT room? . . .

The poet Seamus Heaney likes to make us use all our senses. He was born on a farm in Ireland and many of his poems recall vividly the world of his childhood. If you have ever picked blackberries yourself you will recognise what he describes: if you haven't then the poem may give you a sense of what it is like. As you hear it read ask yourself what senses we need to use in order to share Heaney's experience. Bluebeard, who is mentioned in the poem, by the way, was a murderer.

BLACKBERRY-PICKING

(for Philip Hobsbaum)

Late August, given heavy rain and sun
For a full week, the blackberries would ripen.
At first, just one, a glossy purple clot
Among others, red, green, hard as a knot.
You ate that first one and its flesh was sweet
Like thickened wine: summer's blood was in it
Leaving stains upon the tongue and lust for
Picking. Then red ones inked up and that hunger

Sent us out with milk-cans, pea-tins, jam-pots
Where briars scratched and wet grass bleached our boots.
We trekked and picked until the cans were full,
Until the tinkling bottom had been covered
With green ones, and on top big dark blobs burned
Like a plate of eyes. Our hands were peppered
With thorn pricks, our palms sticky as Bluebeard's.

We hoarded the fresh berries in the byre.
But when the bath was filled we found a fur,
A rat-grey fungus, glutting on our cache.
The juice was stinking too. Once off the bush
The fruit fermented, the sweet flesh would turn sour.
I always felt like crying. It wasn't fair
That all the lovely canfuls smelt of rot.
Each year I hoped they'd keep, knew they would not.

SEAMUS HEANEY

On your own

● Jot down some notes on the following:
— Any words or phrases that stay in your mind's eye, any pictures that you can *see* clearly.
— Any words or phrases that suggest sounds that you might *hear*.
— Any words or phrases that suggest the *touch* or feel of things.
— Any words or phrases that suggest the *smells* Heaney associated with blackberry-picking.
— Any words or phrases that suggest the *tastes* he remembers from the expedition.

In groups

● Compare your ideas and explain your choices.

As well as getting us to use our senses, Seamus Heaney invites us to share his *feelings*. How would you describe his feelings at the beginning of the poem? During the expedition? At the end? How do they change and why do you think they do?

Further Poems

D H Lawrence: 'Baby Running Barefoot'   p. 184
John Agard: 'Poetry Jump-up'   p. 211
Ted Hughes: 'Work and Play'   p. 128

Mixed Feelings

(i) Pictures of feelings

Negative feelings, positive feelings, mixed feelings – this unit looks at a few poems which explore different feelings. Haiku poems are a good place to start because their smallness means that they usually focus upon a single feeling. In the following three haiku we both see a scene in our mind's eye and know whether the writer feels joy, sadness, surprise or anything else about it.

In pairs

● Read through the poems and discuss them with your partner.

IN THE HOUSE

At the butterflies
the caged bird gazes, envying –
just watch its eyes!

ISSA

PARTING

For me who go,
for you who stay –
two autumns.

BUSON

THE LITTLE DUCK

'I've just come from a place
at the lake bottom!' — *that* is the look
on the little duck's face.

JOSO

● In the first poem, what are the feelings of the caged bird? Why does the poet refer to its eyes?

- In 'Parting' what is the feeling expressed by the phrase 'two autumns'?
- In the third poem what is the look on the duck's face? What does its supposed remark on surfacing tell us about how it feels?

On your own

One way to focus on pictures of feelings is to try 'list poems'. Everyone feels excited or bored, lonely or frightened at some time or other – as well as a host of other things as well. Take one feeling you have fairly often – loneliness, excitement, boredom, fear, and simply list five or six objects or scenes that you associate with it. Begin your list 'Loneliness is . . .', or 'Fear is. . . ' and write down each phrase on a separate line. Here is an example.

The poet Adrian Henri begins his poem 'Love is . . .' like this:

Love is . . .

Love is feeling cold in the back of vans
Love is a fanclub with only two fans
Love is walking holding paintstained hands
Love is

Each verse of the poem follows the same pattern. Have a go on your own first. Then, if several of the class have chosen the same feeling, you could get together in groups and combine the best bits of writing into a longer group poem to be illustrated and displayed.

(ii) Mixed feelings

Feelings are often difficult to explain and sometimes unexpected.

As a class

- Why do people enjoy watching a sad play or film or reading a sad book or poem? Why does somebody explain 'I'm crying because I'm so happy'? Are there are any villains in films or plays that you 'love to hate'? How is it possible to enjoy being frightened by a horror film? Share your ideas and see how far you agree.
- Sometimes, perhaps more often than not, our feelings are complicated – we have 'mixed feelings' – as the writer of the next poem discovered. Listen to it read aloud.

THE LESSON

'Your father's gone,' my bald headmaster said.
His shiny dome and brown tobacco jar
Splintered at once in tears. It wasn't grief.
I cried for knowledge which was bitterer
Than any grief. For there and then I knew
That grief has uses — that a father dead
Could bind the bully's fist a week or two;
And then I cried for shame, then for relief.

I was a month past ten when I learnt this:
I still remember how the noise was stilled
In school-assembly when my grief came in.
Some goldfish in a bowl quietly sculled
Around their shining prison on its shelf.
They were indifferent. All the other eyes
Were turned towards me. Somewhere in myself
Pride, like a goldfish, flashed a sudden fin.

EDWARD LUCIE-SMITH

— What does the boy do when he first hears of his father's death?
— Why?
— How do his feelings change?
— Why does he feel pride?

Although these feelings are not perhaps what we might expect a child to feel at the death of a parent, can you understand them? What do they tell us about this ten year old boy?

On your own

Feelings are often contradictory things. Most people have felt guilty about not feeling what they are supposed to feel – at the death of a relative perhaps, or at the way they react to the news of a tragedy or to an Oxfam advertisement.

● If there is an incident that has given you mixed feelings, write it out as a narrative poem and include in your story what you felt about the events.

As a class

Finally, here is a poem that challenges our feelings and, perhaps, makes us rather uncomfortable. As you hear it read aloud, ask yourself why this might be so.

Roger McGough explores the feelings of a photographer who accepts commissions to photograph everything from glossy adverts to starving children.

THE COMMISSION

In this poem there is a table
Groaning with food.
There is also a child
Groaning for lack of food.
The food is beautifully photographed
The meat more succulent
The fruit as juicy
As you are likely to see.
(The child is sketched in lightly
She is not important.)
The photograph is to be used
In a glossy magazine
As part of a campaign
Advertising after-dinner mints.

This evening the photographer
In receipt of his fee
Celebrates by dining with friends
In a famous West End restaurant.
Doodling on the napkin between courses
The photographer, always creative,
Draws a little Asian girl,
Naked, wide-eyed, pleading.
He has an idea for the next commission.
The one for famine relief.
The tandoori arrives
He puts away his pen
And picks up a fork.

● The tone of the poem is deliberately matter-of-fact, almost lacking in feeling you might think at first sight. Is it? What does it make *you* feel?

Further Poems

PART B

Ten
Themes

Word-pictures

MOON MAGIC

Leading me along,
my shadow goes back home
from looking at the moon.

SODO

SPRING

They have the guise
of being married just today –
those two butterflies.

RYOTA

TOPS

Tops heel and yaw,
Sent newly spinning:
Squirm round the floor
At the beginning,
Then draw gravely up
Like candle-flames, till
They are soundless, asleep,
Moving, yet still.
So they run on,
Until, with a falter,
A flicker – soon gone –
Their pace starts to alter:
Heeling again
As if hopelessly tired
They wobble, and then
The poise we admired
Reels, clatters and sprawls,
Pathetically over.
– And what most appals
Is that tiny first shiver,
That stumble, whereby
We know beyond doubt
They have almost run out
And are starting to die.

PHILIP LARKIN

HEAT

The summer river:
although there is a bridge, my horse
goes through the water.

SHIKI

CROW

On a withered branch
a crow has settled –
autumn nightfall.

BASHO

THE RED COCKATOO

Sent as a present from Annam—
A red cockatoo.
Coloured like the peach-tree blossom,
Speaking with the speech of men.
And they did to it what is always done
To the learned and eloquent.
They took a cage with stout bars
And shut it up inside.

PO CHU-I
(Trans. Arthur Waley)

WATER PICTURE

In the pond in the park
all things are doubled:
Long buildings hang and
wriggle gently. Chimneys
are bent legs bouncing
on clouds below. A flag
wags like a fishhook
down there in the sky.

The arched stone bridge
is an eye, with underlid
in the water. In its lens
dip crinkled heads with hats
that don't fall off. Dogs go by,
barking on their backs.
A baby, taken to feed the
ducks, dangles upside-down,
a pink balloon for a buoy.

Treetops deploy a haze of
cherry bloom for roots,
where birds coast belly-up
in the glass bowl of a hill;
from its bottom a bunch
of peanut-munching children
is suspended by their
sneakers, waveringly.

A swan, with twin necks
forming the figure three,
steers between two dimpled
towers doubled. Fondly
hissing, she kisses herself,
and all the scene is troubled:
water-windows splinter,
tree-limbs tangle, the bridge
folds like a fan.

MAY SWENSON

THE EXCAVATION

Clusters of electric bulbs
Like giant chrysanthemums
Paint the black cavern
With streaks and blots
Of faded yellow.
In grotesque mimicry
The monstrous shadows
Ape each movement of toiling men.
The stale pungent odour of unpacked earth
Tickles the nostrils.
Through the wood-plank roof
The dull-booming rumble
Of scampering traffic
Trickles in—

But is swallowed up
By the harsh purr of the drill
As it bites frenziedly
Into the dogged rock.

Overhead, unseen,
A mountain of stone is kept upright
By a slender steel beam
And a theory.

MAX ENDICOFF

THE COVETOUS MAN

These lines are from an imaginary story of a ploughman who has a
dream in which he travels round the world seeing all kinds of bad
behaviour, particularly from members of the church. On his journey,
Piers the ploughman meets each of the Seven Deadly Sins who are
pictured as people.

And thanne cam Coveitise. Can I him nought
                descrive,
So hungriliche and holwe sire Hervy him looked.*
He was bitelbrowed and baberlipped also,*
With two blered eyghen as a blinde hagge;
And as a letheren purs lolled his chekes,
Wel sidder than his chin* they chiveled for elde;*
And as a bondman* of his bacoun his berde was
                bidraveled;*
With an hoode on his hed, a lousy* hatte above,
And in a tawny tabarde of twelve winter age,
Al totorne and baudy* and ful of lis creepinge;
But if that a lous couthe have lopen* the bettre,
She sholde noughte have walked on that welche,*
           so was it thredebare.

* he looked hungrily and gaunt like Sir Harvey (nickname for a greedy cheat)
* beetle-browed and blubber-lipped

* hanging lower than his chin
* quivered with age
* like a servant or labourer
* bedraggled with bacon grease
* louse-ridden

* torn and dirty
* unless a louse could jump better
* welsh flannel

From, *Piers Plowman,*

WILLIAM LANGLAND, c.1360.

Four Epitaphs

FACTS OF DEATH

The play is over:
You can die now.

G P WALLEY

CHARLES THE SECOND

Here lies our Sovereign Lord the King,
  Whose word no man relies on,
Who never said a foolish thing,
  Nor ever did a wise one.

JOHN WILMOT

ON A PESSIMIST

I'm Smith of Stoke, aged sixty-odd,
  I've lived without a dame
From youth-time on; and would to God
  My dad had done the same.

THOMAS HARDY
(*from the French and Greek*)

MATTHEW BIRD

I, the Reverend Matthew Bird,
Preacher of God's Holy Word,
Taking leave of aisle and pew,
Go to find how much is true.

L A G STRONG

Haiku Remind yourself of the 5–7–5 haiku syllable pattern (p. 3). Think about this advice from one of Japan's greatest haiku poets, Shiki:

'Remember perspective. Large things are large, but small things are also large if seen close up...
Keep the words tight; put in nothing useless.
Cut down as much as possible on adverbs and verbs.
Use both imaginary pictures and real ones, but prefer the real ones'.

In pairs

- Note down and talk about a few things which you can study closely – a leaf? an insect? a stamp? – perhaps with the aid of a magnifying glass. Discuss the details and jot down any words or phrases or comparisons that come to mind. Then, each of you choose *one* of the objects from your list and, when writing your haiku about it, try to take Shiki's advice.

Definitions

Our ideas about big, complicated issues can often be defined quite sharply in terms of word–pictures.

Students of about of your own age defined Death as

'beyond the night without your father'

and Fear as

'a very dark room with very white curtains'.

On your own

- Attempt your own definitions of some of the following: Time, Beginning, Insincerity, Evil, Fear, Death, Hunger, Love, Loneliness, Wisdom, Happiness.

Reflections

On your own

- Re-read May Swenson's 'Water Picture' (p. 57) and think about how you could write a sequel. Reflections in water often produce strange effects because things seen at different levels merge into each other. If you imagine looking down from a bridge into slow-moving water you might see objects on the surface – floating litter, water-flies, oil slicks; then perhaps, the reflections of yourself and your surroundings. Next, you may pick out sediment, weed, perhaps fish – things moving in the water; and, at the deepest level, perhaps you can make out the stones, tin-cans and other debris on the bottom. Make a list of all the things you see on the surface, suspended in the water, and on the river bed. Write up your list into a descriptive poem. Illustrate it if you can.

Comparisons

In pairs

● Jot down as many different comparisons as you can which are suggested by the following: clouds building up on the horizon; a snowflake; smoke billowing from chimneys; balloons – tethered or free; the back of your hand; soapsuds; raindrops on a window; frogspawn or tadpoles; frost on a window pane. Talk about these with your partner. Then choose one or two of your comparisons as the basis for making a short poem. If several of you have written good descriptions of, say, balloons, see if you can link them together into a longer poem, or 'tie' them together into a design.

Thumbnail Sketch

On your own

● Look back at Ezra Pound's two-line poem 'In a Station of the Metro' (p. 5) which was reduced from a longer first draft. Using *one* of the three poems, 'The Excavation', 'Tops' or 'Water Picture' (pp. 56–58) as your first draft, write your own two-line poem on the same subject. For instance, if you choose 'The Excavation', you might describe the building site as:

'Men tangled in the arc lights' glare;
Yellow ants toiling in their dark nest.'

Epitaphs

In pairs/on your own

● There are epitaphs on p. 59 for a king and a preacher. Invent suitable epitaphs for people in other occupations: a rock star, a mother, a teacher, a bank manager....

Personification

In pairs

● Look back at pp. 12–13 to remind yourself of how ideas can be pictured as people. Now, read 'The Covetous Man' (p. 58) and, with the help of the footnotes, translate it into modern English. Which version do you prefer and why?

Shapes and Sounds

SNOWFLAKE

Little shaving
of hot white cold
Snowflake
Snowflake
you really bold

How you feeling, Snowflake?
Icily-Hot
How you feeling, Snowflake?
Ice-Silly-Hot

Snowflake
Snowflake
you little clown

c
  a
    r
    n
  i
  v
   a
    l
     l
      i
     n
     g

     d
     o
     w
      n

A small ghost kiss
on my warm tongue.

GRACE NICHOLS

TO A SNOWFLAKE

What heart could have thought you?—
Past our devisal
(O filigree petal!)
Fashioned so purely,
Fragilely, surely,
From what Paradisal
Imagineless metal,
Too costly for cost?
Who hammered you, wrought you,
From argentine★ vapour?—   ★silvery
'God was my shaper.
Passing surmisal,
He hammered, He wrought me,
From curled silver vapour,
To lust of His mind:—
Thou couldst not have thought me!
So purely, so palely,
Tinily, surely,
Mightily, frailly,
Insculpted and embossed,
With His hammer of wind,
And His graver of frost.'

FRANCIS THOMPSON

one

t
hi
s

snowflake

(a
   li
     ght
   in
g)

is upon a gra

v
es
t

one

E. E. CUMMINGS

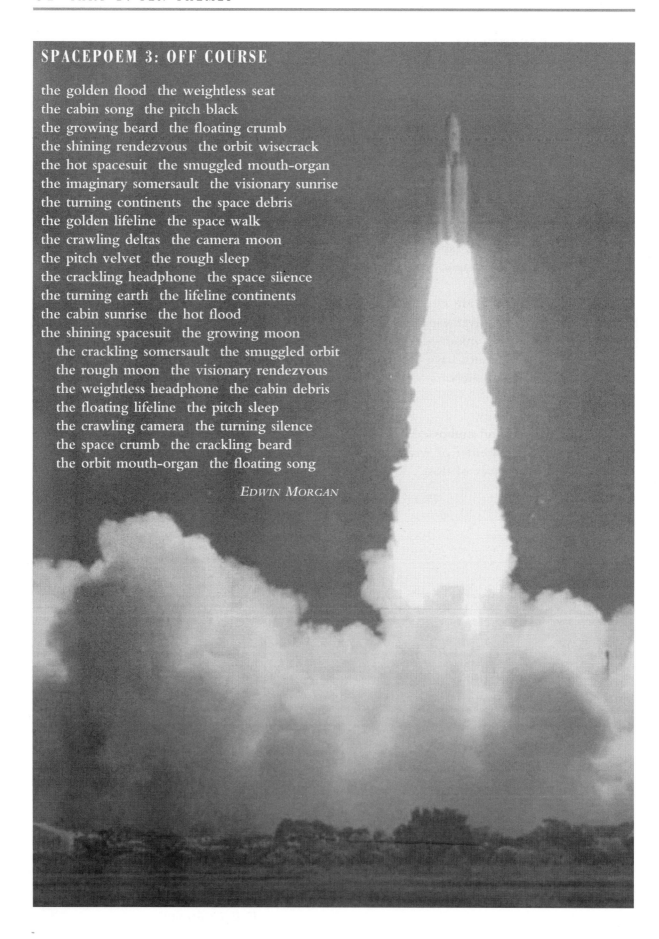

SPACEPOEM 3: OFF COURSE

the golden flood the weightless seat
the cabin song the pitch black
the growing beard the floating crumb
the shining rendezvous the orbit wisecrack
the hot spacesuit the smuggled mouth-organ
the imaginary somersault the visionary sunrise
the turning continents the space debris
the golden lifeline the space walk
the crawling deltas the camera moon
the pitch velvet the rough sleep
the crackling headphone the space silence
the turning earth the lifeline continents
the cabin sunrise the hot flood
the shining spacesuit the growing moon
   the crackling somersault the smuggled orbit
   the rough moon the visionary rendezvous
   the weightless headphone the cabin debris
   the floating lifeline the pitch sleep
   the crawling camera the turning silence
   the space crumb the crackling beard
   the orbit mouth-organ the floating song

EDWIN MORGAN

THE COMPUTER'S FIRST CHRISTMAS CARD

```
j  o  l  l  y  m  e  r  r  y
h  o  l  l  y  b  e  r  r  y
j  o  l  l  y  b  e  r  r  y
m  e  r  r  y  h  o  l  l  y
h  a  p  p  y  j  o  l  l  y
j  o  l  l  y  j  e  l  l  y
j  e  l  l  y  b  e  l  l  y
b  e  l  l  y  m  e  r  r  y
h  o  l  l  y  h  e  p  p  y
j  o  l  l  y  M  o  l  l  y
m  a  r  r  y  J  e  r  r  y
m  e  r  r  y  H  a  r  r  y
h  o  p  p  y  B  a  r  r  y
h  e  p  p  y  J  a  r  r  y
b  o  p  p  y  h  e  p  p  y
b  e  r  r  y  j  o  r  r  y
j  o  r  r  y  j  o  l  l  y
m  o  p  p  y  j  e  l  l  y
M  o  l  l  y  m  e  r  r  y
J  e  r  r  y  j  o  l  l  y
b  e  l  l  y  b  o  p  p  y
j  o  r  r  y  h  o  p  p  y
h  o  l  l  y  m  o  p  p  y
B  a  r  r  y  m  e  r  r  y
J  a  r  r  y  h  a  p  p  y
h  a  p  p  y  b  o  p  p  y
b  o  p  p  y  j  o  l  l  y
j  o  l  l  y  m  e  r  r  y
m  e  r  r  y  m  e  r  r  y
m  e  r  r  y  m  e  r  r  y
m  e  r  r  y  C  h  r  i  s
a  m  m  e  r  r  y  a  s  a
C  h  r  i  s  m  e  r  r  y
a  s  M  E  R  R  Y  C  H  R
Y  S  A  N  T  H  E  M  U  M
```

EDWIN MORGAN

CAT

To plan plan to create to have
whiskers cool carat silver ready and curved
bristling

to plan plan to create to have
eyes green doors that dilate greenest
pouncers

to be ready rubber ball ready
feet bouncers cool fluid in
tension

to be steady steady claws all
attention to wait wait and create
pouncing

to be a cat eeling through alleys
slipping through windows of odours
to feel swiftness slowly

to halt at the gate hearing
unlocking whispers paper feet wrapping
potatoes and papers

to hear nicely mice spider feet
scratching great horny nails
catching a fire flies wire legs etch-

ing yet stretching beyond this arch
untriumphant lazily rubb-
ing the soft fur of home

EDWARD KAMAU BRATHWAITE

CATS

Cats sleep
Anywhere,
Any table,
Any chair,
Top of piano,
Window-ledge,
In the middle,
On the edge,
Open drawer,
Empty shoe,
Anybody's
Lap will do,
Fitted in a
Cardboard box,
In the cupboard
With your frocks—
Anywhere!
They don't care!
Cats sleep
Anywhere.

ELEANOR FARJEON

LIMBO DANCER'S MANTRA*

* A word that is said or chanted as an incantation or magic spell.

LIMB/BOW

Pronounce dem
two syllable
real slow
you hear me
real slow

LIMB/BOW

Savour dem
two syllable
till glow
spread from head
to tip of toe

LIMB/BOW

Contemplate dem
two syllable
in vertigo
of drum tempo

LIMBO

Meditate on dem
two syllable
calm as zero
vibrate to sound
let mind go

and forget the stick
I tell you
don't think about the stick

that will take care of itself

                    JOHN AGARD

The poems in this section are all chosen because the way the words are arranged on the page suggests how we might read them. The shape and the sound help each other.

Writing The poem on p. 62 by Grace Nichols suggests, by the way the words are laid out on the page, the lazy, wavering fall of a single snowflake.

On your own

● Think of other things – falling leaves; a feather drifting to the ground; a sky-rocket soaring, bursting, falling; the sense of movement and not movement as you drop in a lift; a diver arching into the water from a high board – which you could write about in a similar way. Choose one and write your own shape poem.

Performing and Writing 1

'The Computer's First Christmas Card' on p. 65 is arranged to suggest a mad computer print out running out of control down the page.

In groups

● Practise a reading of the poem. The best readings are usually those which are very serious and mechanical and don't see anything remotely odd in the strange words that spill out.

On your own

● Think about other poems that this computer might write and what they could look like. What might this computer print as Baby's First Birthday Card? a Happy New Year card, or a Get Well Soon card? When you are happy with your idea you might word process your new poem.

Performing and writing 2

Edwin Morgan's 'Spacepoem 3: Off Course' (p. 64) is written so that the random set of images to do with space travel with which he begins the poem, steadily disintegrates and the words pair up with each other in different combinations – almost as though they are floating away into space – off course, in fact.

In groups

- Practise a reading of the poem which suggests the strange, dreamlike tone of the poem. You might choose to give each phrase to a different voice – but there are many ways of presenting your reading.

On your own

- Edwin Morgan has assembled about 17 perfectly normal phrases that might come from a report on a space mission before he lets them start to re-assemble themselves into strange and unexpected patterns. Take a situation such as going to sleep; daydreaming in class; going under anaesthetic in hospital or at the dentists (and waking up) – and assemble a group of normal phrases which you then allow to drift together in a dreamlike way as Edwin Morgan has done. Work them up into a poem of the same kind.

Performing 1

Eleanor Farjeon's poem 'Cats' on p. 66 suggests something of the delicate movement of the cat. The short lines and neat little rhymes are in tune with the preciseness of the cat in its choice of sleeping place. Edward Kamau Brathwaite's *Cat* poem suggests something of the same fastidiousness in the cat but there is a scheming intelligence and maybe a little cruelty about it.

In groups

- Prepare a reading of Eleanor Farjeon's poem using several voices. You can, if you like, split it so that each line is taken by a different voice. Think carefully about what is the right tone to adopt. Present your reading to the rest of the class.
- Prepare a reading of Brathwaite's cat poem. It is more difficult and you will notice that there is no punctuation at all to guide you. The last three verses need some thought. You could split the poem between four voices, each taking alternate verses. Try to feel the tension that is always present in the cat in the main part of the poem and contrast it with the softness of the last verse.

Performing 2

- Before you read John Agard's poem 'Limbo Dancer's Mantra' on p. 67, look at the description of the limbo dance on p. 42 (and maybe read Edward Brathwaite's poem as well). You could try reading the poem with one voice taking the main verses and the class quietly but forcefully chanting the one word LIMB/BOW. John Agard spells 'Limbo' as he does partly to make us pronounce it very powerfully: the spelling also suggests something else perhaps. (Think of the movement).

Ballads

THE TWA CORBIES*

*Two crows

As I was walking all alone,
I heard twa corbies making a moan:
The one unto the other say,
'Where shall we gang and dine today?'

'In behind yon auld fail* dyke   *turf
I wot there lies a new slain knight;
And nobody kens that he lies there,
But his hawk, his hound and his lady fair.

'His hound is to the hunting gane,
His hawk to fetch the wild fowl hame,
His lady's ta'en another mate,
So we may make our dinner sweet.

'Ye'll sit upon his white hause-bane*   *collar-bone
And I'll pike out his bonny blue een;
And with one lock of his golden hair
We'll theek* our nest when it grows bare.   *line

'Many a one for him makes moan,
But none shall ken where he is gone;
O'er his white bones when they are bare,
The wind shall blow for evermair.'

ANON

THE UNQUIET GRAVE

'The wind doth blow today, my love,
   And a few small drops of rain;
I never had but one true-love,
   In a cold grave she was lain.

'I'll do as much for my true-love
   As any young man may;
I'll sit and mourn all at her grave
   For a twelvemonth and a day.'

The twelvemonth and a day being up,
   The dead began to speak:
'Oh who sits weeping on my grave,
   And will not let me sleep?'

''Tis I, my love, sits on your grave,
   And will not let you sleep;
For I crave one kiss of your clay-cold lips,
   And that is all I seek.'

'You crave one kiss of my clay-cold lips;
   But my breath smells earthy strong;
If you have one kiss of my clay-cold lips,
   Your time will not be long.

''Tis down in yonder garden green,
   Love, where we used to walk,
The finest flower that ere was seen
   Is withered to a stalk.

'The stalk is withered dry my love,
   So will our hearts decay;
So make yourself content, my love,
   Till God calls you away.'

ANON

THE CHERRY-TREE CAROL

Joseph was an old man,
  An old man was he
When he wedded Mary
  In the land of Galilee.

Joseph and Mary walking
  In the midst of a wood
Saw berries and cherries
  As red as the blood.

O then bespoke Mary,
  So meek and so mild,
'Pray get me one cherry,
  For I am with child.'

O then bespoke Joseph,
  So rude and unkind,
'Let him get thee a cherry
  That got thee with child.'

O then bespoke the babe
  Within his mother's womb,
'Bow down, thou tall cherry-tree,
  And give my mother some.'

Then bowed down the tall cherry-tree
  To his mother's right hand,
And she cried, 'See, Joseph,
  I have cherries at command!'

And Mary ate her cherry
  As red as the blood;
Then Mary went on
  With her heavy load.

                    ANON

MOTHER AND MAIDEN

I sing of a maiden
  That is matchless.
King of all kings
  For her son she chose.

He came all so still
  Where his mother was,
As dew in April
  That falleth on the grass.

He came all so still
  To his mother's bower,
As dew in April
  That falleth on the flower.

He came all so still—
  There his mother lay,
As dew in April
  That falleth on the spray.

Mother and maiden
  Was never none but she;
Well may such a lady
  God's mother be.

                    ANON

THE DEMON LOVER

'O where have you been, my long, long love,
   This long seven years and more?'
'O I'm come to seek my former vows
   Ye granted me before.'

'O hold your tongue of your former vows,
   For they will breed sad strife;
O hold your tongue of your former vows
   For I am become a wife.'

He turned him right and round about,
   And the tear blinded his ee:
'I would never hae trodden on Irish ground,
   If it had not been for thee.

'I might hae had a king's daughter,
   Far, far beyond the sea;
I might have had a king's daughter,
   Had it not been for love o' thee.'

'If ye might have had a king's daughter,
   Yeself ye had to blame;
Ye might have taken the king's daughter,
   For ye kend* that I was nane.†   *knew †none

'If I was to leave my husband dear,
   And my two babes also,
O what have you to take me to,
   If with you I should go?'

'I have seven ships upon the sea—
   And the eighth brought me to land—
With four-and-twenty bold mariners,
   And music on every hand.'

She has taken up her two little babes,
   Kissed them both cheek and chin:
'O fare ye well, my own two babes,
   For I'll never see you again.'

She set her foot upon the ship,
  No mariners could she behold;
But the sails were made of taffeta,
  And the masts of beaten gold.

She had not sailed a league, a league,
  A league but barely three,
When dismal grew his countenance,
  And drumlie★ grew his ee.†   ★gloomy, murky †eye

They had not sailed a league, a league,
  A league but barely three,
Until she espied his cloven foot,
  And she wept right bitterly.

'O hold your tongue of your weeping,' says he,
  'Of your weeping now let me be;
I will shew you how the lilies grow
  On the banks of Italy.'

'O what hills are yon, yon pleasant hills,
  That the sun shines sweetly on?'
'O yon are the hills of heaven,' he said,
  'Where you will never win.'

'O whaten★ a mountain is yon,' she said,   ★what sort of
  'All so dreary with frost and snow?'
'O yon is the mountain of hell,' he cried,
  'Where you and I will go.'

He struck the top-mast with his hand,
  The fore-mast with his knee,
And he broke that gallant ship in twain,
  And sank her in the sea.

ANON

THE BALLAD OF CHARLOTTE DYMOND

It was a Sunday evening
And in the April rain
That Charlotte went from our house
And never came home again.

Her shawl of diamond redcloth
She wore a yellow gown,
She carried the green gauze handkerchief
She bought in Bodmin town.

About her throat her necklace
And in her purse her pay:
The four silver shillings
She had at Lady Day.

In her purse four shillings
And in her purse her pride.
As she walked out one evening
Her lover at her side.

Out beyond the marshes
Where the cattle stand,
With her crippled lover
Limping at her hand.

Charlotte walked with Matthew
Through the Sunday mist,
Never saw the razor
Waiting at his wrist.

Charlotte she was gentle
But they found her in the flood
Her Sunday beads among the reeds
Beaming with her blood.

Matthew, where is Charlotte,
And wherefore has she flown?
For you walked out together
And now are come alone.

Why do you not answer,
Stand silent as a tree,
Your Sunday worsted stockings
All muddied to the knee?

Why do you mend your breast-pleat
With a rusty needle's thread
And fall with fears and silent tears
Upon your single bed?

Why do you sit so sadly
Your face the colour of clay
And with a green gauze handkerchief
Wipe the sour sweat away?

Has she gone to Blisland
To seek an easier place?
And is that why your eye won't dry
And blinds your bleaching face?

'Take me home!' cried Charlotte,
'I lie here in the pit!'
A red rock rests upon my breasts
And my naked neck is split!'

Her skin was soft as sable
Her eyes were wide as day,
Her hair was blacker than the bog
That licked her life away.

Her cheeks were made of honey,
Her throat was made of flame
Where all around the razor
Had written its red name.

As Matthew turned at Plymouth
About the tilting Hoe,
The cold and cunning Constable
Up to him did go.

'I've come to take you, Matthew,
Unto the Magistrate's door.
Come quiet now, you pretty poor boy,
And you must know what for.'

'She is as pure,' cried Matthew,
'As is the early dew,
Her only stain it is the pain
That round her neck I drew!

'She is as guiltless as the day
She sprang forth from her mother.
The only sin upon her skin
Is that she loved another.'

They took him off to Bodmin,
They pulled the prison bell,
They sent him smartly up to heaven
And dropped him down to Hell.

All through the granite kingdom
And on its travelling airs
Ask which of these two lovers
The most deserves your prayers.

And your steel heart search, Stranger
That you may pause and pray
For lovers who come not to bed
Upon their wedding day.

But lie upon the moorland
Where stands the sacred snow
Above the breathing river,
And the salt sea-winds go.

CHARLES CAUSLEY

ALTERNATIVE ENDINGS TO AN UNWRITTEN BALLAD

I stole through the dungeons, while everyone slept,
    Till I came to the cage where the Monster was kept.
There, locked in the arms of a Giant Baboon,
    Rigid and smiling, lay ... MRS RAVOON!

I climbed the clock-tower in the first morning sun
    And 'twas midday at least ere my journey was done;
But the clock never sounded the last stroke of noon,
    For there, from the clapper, swung MRS RAVOON.

I hauled in the line, and I took my first look
    At the half-eaten horror that hung from the hook.
I had dragged from the depths of the limpid lagoon
    The luminous body of MRS RAVOON.

I fled in the tempest, through lightning and thunder,
    And there, as a flash split the darkness asunder,
Chewing a rat's-tail and mumbling a rune,
    Mad in the moat squatted MRS RAVOON.

I stood by the waters so green and so thick,
  And I stirred at the scum with my old, withered stick;
When there rose through the ooze, like a monstrous balloon,
  The bloated cadaver of MRS RAVOON.

Facing the fens, I looked back from the shore
  Where all had been empty a moment before;
And there, by the light of the Lincolnshire moon,
  Immense on the marshes stood ... MRS RAVOON!

PAUL DEHN

Performing 1

The ballad of 'The Twa Corbies' (p. 70) tells of two carrion crows contemplating feeding off the body of a newly slain knight. Notice how all the images in the ballad are simple, direct, and imprint themselves on the mind's eye: the black crows, the white bones, the blue eyes and golden hair are all very striking. It is a traditional Scottish ballad and written in dialect. Try reading it aloud. You could work in threes and have the voices of a narrator (at the beginning) and two crows. The first crow asks only 'Where shall we gang (go) and dine today?' but you could give the last two verses to the first crow instead of the second if you want to even up the reading.

Performing and writing 1

Charlotte Dymond was a young Cornish girl who was tragically murdered by her lover, Matthew, because he believed she loved another. Charles Causley uses the old ballad form when he re-tells her story (p. 75). Listen to the poem being read through once and then, in groups, divide up the poem and produce your own reading of it with different voices taking different parts.

On your own

● You might like to tackle writing your own ballad: it isn't as difficult as it may seem. Charlotte Dymond's story is sadly similar to so many stories that appear in newspapers every day. Take a story from a newspaper and try to tell it simply in verses of four lines each. Aim to make the last words of the second and fourth lines rhyme in each verse if you can.

Performing and writing 2

In his poem 'Alternative Endings to an Unwritten Ballad' (p. 76)
Paul Dehn writes six possible last verses to a poem he in fact never
wrote. Five of the verses end with the ghastly death of his imagined
character Mrs Ravoon: in the sixth she gets a new lease of life. In
groups read a verse each and see who can produce the most horrifying
rendering of this melodramatic tale.

On your own/In pairs

- Either write your own Mrs Ravoon verse (tricky as Dehn has used all
  the obvious rhyming words except 'soon' and 'boon' though there are
  close rhymes like 'strewn'). Or write your own verses for a character
  with another name – 'Mr O'Toole' perhaps or 'Old granny Green'. Or, if
  you are really ambitious, try writing a story that would end
  appropriately with one of Paul Dehn's verses.

Performing 2

The ballad of 'The Demon Lover' (p. 73) is an old Scottish tale that
deals with a favourite theme of the ballad makers – the spirit returned
from the dead. Read the poem through carefully and discuss what
happens. Decide on the main turning points in the story.

In groups

- Prepare a reading of the poem: three voices are needed – those of the
  young wife, the spirit of her lover and the narrator.

THE HISTORY OF THE FLOOD

Bang Bang Bang
Said the nails in the Ark.

It's getting rather dark
Said the nails in the Ark.

For the rain is coming down
Said the nails in the Ark.

And you're all like to drown
Said the nails in the Ark.

Dark and black as sin
Said the nails in the Ark.

So won't you all come in
Said the nails in the Ark.

But only two by two
Said the nails in the Ark.

So they came in two by two,
The elephant, the kangaroo,
And the gnu,
And the little tiny shrew.

Then the birds
Flocked in like winged words:
Two racket-tailed motmots, two macaws,
Two nuthatches and two
Little bright robins.

And the reptiles: the gila monster, the slow-worm,
The green mamba, the cottonmouth and the alligator—
All squirmed in;
And after a very lengthy walk,
Two giant Galapagos tortoises.

And the insects in their hierarchies:
A queen ant, a king ant, a queen wasp, a king wasp,
A queen bee, a king bee,
And all the beetles, bugs and mosquitoes,
Cascaded in like glittering, murmurous jewels.

But the fish had their wish;
For the rain came down.
People began to drown:
The wicked, the rich—
They gasped out bubbles of pure gold,
Which exhalations
Rose to the constellations.

So for forty days and forty nights
They were on the waste of waters
In those cramped quarters.
It was very dark, damp and lonely.
There was nothing to see, but only
The rain which continued to drop.
It did not stop.

So Noah sent forth a Raven.
The raven said 'Kark!
I will not go back to the Ark.'
The raven was footloose,
He fed on the bodies of the rich—
Rich with vitamins and goo.
They had become bloated,
And everywhere they floated.

The raven's heart was black,
He did not come back.

It was not a nice thing to do:
Which is why the raven is a token of wrath,
And creaks like a rusty gate
When he crosses your path; and Fate
Will grant you no luck that day:
The raven is fey:
You were meant to have a scare.
Fortunately in England
The raven is rather rare.

Then Noah sent forth a dove
She did not want to rove.
She longed for her love—
The other turtle dove—
(For her no other dove!)
She brought back a twig from an olive-tree.
There is no more beautiful tree
Anywhere on the earth,
Even when it comes to birth
From six weeks under the sea.

She did not want to rove.
She wanted to take her rest,
And to build herself a nest
All in the olive grove.
She wanted to make love.
She thought that was the best

The dove was not a rover;
So they knew that the rain was over.
Noah and his wife got out
(They had become rather stout)
And Japhet, Ham and Shem.
(The same could be said of them.)
They looked up at the sky.
The earth was becoming dry.

Then the animals came ashore—
There were more of them than before:
There were two dogs and a litter of puppies;
There were a tom-cat and two tib-cats
And two litters of kittens—cats
Do not obey regulations;
And, as you might expect,
A quantity of rabbits.

God put a rainbow in the sky.
They wondered what it was for.
There had never been a rainbow before.
The rainbow was a sign;
It looked like a neon sign—
Seven colours arched in the skies:
What should it publicize?
They looked up with wondering eyes.

It advertises Mercy
Said the nails in the Ark.

Mercy Mercy Mercy
Said the nails in the Ark.

Our God is merciful
Said the nails in the Ark.

Merciful and gracious
Bang Bang Bang Bang.

JOHN HEATH-STUBBS

THE RIME OF THE ANCIENT MARINER*

*This is a slightly shortened version of Coleridge's poem. Most of the omissions are from the last three parts of the poem.

PART I

It is an ancient Mariner,
And he stoppeth one of three.
'By thy long grey beard and glittering eye,
Now wherefore stopp'st thou me?

The Bridegroom's doors are opened wide,
And I am next of kin;
The guests are met, the feast is set:
May'st hear the merry din.'

He holds him with his skinny hand,
'There was a ship,' quoth he.
'Hold off! unhand me, grey-beard loon!'
Eftsoons his hand dropt he.

He holds him with his glittering eye—
The Wedding-Guest stood still,
And listens like a three years' child:
The Mariner hath his will.

The Wedding-Guest sat on a stone:
He cannot choose but hear;
And thus spake on that ancient man,
The bright-eyed Mariner.

'The ship was cheered, the harbour cleared,
Merrily did we drop
Below the kirk, below the hill,
Below the lighthouse top.

The Sun came up upon the left,
Out of the sea came he!
And he shone bright, and on the right
Went down into the sea.

Higher and higher every day,
Till over the mast at noon—'
The Wedding-Guest here beat his breast,
For he heard the loud bassoon.

'And now the Storm-blast came, and he
Was tyrannous and strong:
He struck with his o'ertaking wings,
And chased us south along.

With sloping masts and dipping prow,
As who pursued with yell and blow
Still treads the shadow of his foe,
And forward bends his head,
The ship drove fast, loud roared the blast,
And southward aye we fled.

And now there came both mist and snow,
And it grew wondrous cold:
And ice, mast-high, came floating by,
As green as emerald.

And through the drifts the snowy clifts
Did send a dismal sheen:
Nor shapes of men nor beasts we ken—
The ice was all between.

The ice was here, the ice was there,
The ice was all around:
It cracked and growled, and roared and
  howled,
Like noises in a swound!

At length did cross an Albatross,
Through the fog it came;
As if it had been a Christian soul,
We hailed it in God's name.

It ate the food it ne'er had eat,
And round and round it flew.
The ice did split with a thunder-fit;
The helmsman steered us through!

And a good south wind sprung up behind;
The Albatross did follow,
And every day, for food or play,
Came to the mariners' hollo!

In mist or cloud, on mast or shroud,
It perched for vespers nine;
Whiles all the night, through fog-smoke white,
Glimmered the white moon-shine.'

'God save thee, ancient Mariner!
From the fiends, that plague thee thus!—
Why look'st thou so?' — 'With my cross-bow
I shot the Albatross.'

PART II
'The Sun now rose upon the right:
Out of the sea came he,
Still hid in mist, and on the left
Went down into the sea.

And the good south wind still blew behind,
But no sweet bird did follow,
Nor any day for food or play
Come to the mariners' hollo!

And I had done a hellish thing,
And it would work 'em woe:
For all averred, I had killed the bird
That made the breeze to blow!
Ah wretch! said they, the bird to slay,
That made the breeze to blow!

Nor dim nor red, like God's own head,
The glorious Sun uprist:
Then all averred, I had killed the bird
That brought the fog and mist.
'Twas right, said they, such birds to slay,
That bring the fog and mist.

The fair breeze blew, the white foam flew,
The furrow followed free;
We were the first that ever burst
Into that silent sea.

Down dropt the breeze, the sails dropt down,
'Twas sad as sad could be;
And we did speak only to break
The silence of the sea!

All in a hot and copper sky,
The bloody Sun, at noon,
Right up above the mast did stand,
No bigger than the Moon.

Day after day, day after day,
We stuck, nor breath nor motion;
As idle as a painted ship
Upon a painted ocean.

Water, water, everywhere,
And all the boards did shrink;
Water, water, everywhere
Nor any drop to drink.

The very deep did rot: O Christ!
That ever this should be!
Yea, slimy things did crawl with legs
Upon the slimy sea.

About, about, in reel and rout
The death-fires danced at night;
The water, like a witch's oils,
Burnt, green and blue and white.

And some in dreams assured were
Of the Spirit that plagued us so;
Nine fathom deep he had followed us
From the land of mist and snow.

And every tongue, through utter drought,
Was withered at the root;
We could not speak, no more than if
We had been choked with soot.

Ah! well a-day! what evil looks
Had I from old and young!
Instead of the cross, the Albatross
About my neck was hung.'

PART III
'There passed a weary time. Each throat
Was parched, and glazed each eye.
A weary time! a weary time!
How glazed each weary eye,
When looking westward, I beheld
A something in the sky.

At first it seemed a little speck,
And then it seemed a mist;
It moved and moved, and took at last
A certain shape, I wist.

A speck, a mist, a shape, I wist!
And still it neared and neared:
As if it dodged a water-sprite,
It plunged and tacked and veered.

With throats unslaked, with black lips baked,
We could nor laugh nor wail;
Through utter drought all dumb we stood!
I bit my arm, I sucked the blood,
And cried, A sail! a sail!

With throats unslaked, with black lips baked,
Agape they heard me call:
Gramercy! they for joy did grin,
And all at once their breath drew in,
As they were drinking all.

See! see! (I cried) she tacks no more!
Hither to work us weal;
Without a breeze, without a tide,
She steadies with upright keel!

The western wave was all a-flame.
The day was well nigh done!
Almost upon the western wave
Rested the broad bright Sun;
When that strange shape drove suddenly
Betwixt us and the Sun.

And straight the Sun was flecked with bars,
(Heaven's Mother send us grace!)
As if through a dungeon-grate he peered
With broad and burning face.

Alas! (thought I, and my heart beat loud)
How fast she nears and nears!
Are those her sails that glance in the Sun,
Like restless gossameres?

Are those her ribs through which the Sun
Did peer, as through a grate?
And is that Woman all her crew?
Is that a Death? and are there two?
Is Death that woman's mate?

Her lips were red, her looks were free,
Her locks were yellow as gold:
Her skin was as white as leprosy,
The Nightmare Life-in-Death was she,
Who thicks man's blood with cold.

The naked hulk alongside came,
And the twain were casting dice:
"The game is done! I've won! I've won."
Quoth she, and whistles thrice.

The Sun's rim dips; the stars rush out:
At one stride comes the dark;
With far-heard whisper, o'er the sea,
Off shot the spectre-bark.

We listened and looked sideways up!
Fear at my heart, as at a cup,
My life-blood seemed to sip!
The stars were dim, and thick the night,
The steersman's face by his lamp gleamed white;
From the sails the dew did drip—
Till clomb above the eastern bar
The horned Moon, with one bright star
Within the nether tip.

One after one, by the star-dogged Moon,
Too quick for groan or sigh,
Each turned his face with a ghastly pang,
And cursed me with his eye.

Four times fifty living men,
(And I heard nor sigh nor groan)
With heavy thump, a lifeless lump,
They dropped down one by one.

The souls did from their bodies fly,—
They fled to bliss or woe!
And every soul, it passed me by,
Like the whizz of my cross-bow!'

PART IV

'I fear thee, ancient Mariner!
I fear thy skinny hand!
And thou art long, and lank, and brown,
As is the ribbed sea-sand.

I fear thee and thy glittering eye,
And thy skinny hand, so brown.'—
'Fear not, fear not, thou Wedding-Guest!
This body dropt not down.

Alone, alone, all, all alone,
Alone on a wide wide sea!
And never a saint took pity on
My soul in agony.

The many men, so beautiful!
And they all dead did lie:
And a thousand thousand slimy things
Lived on; and so did I.

I looked upon the rotting sea,
And drew my eyes away;
I looked upon the rotting deck,
And there the dead men lay.

I looked to heaven, and tried to pray;
But or ever a prayer had gusht,
A wicked whisper came, and made
My heart as dry as dust.

I closed my lids, and kept them close,
And the balls like pulses beat;
For the sky and the sea, and the sea and the sky
Lay like a load on my weary eye,
And the dead were at my feet.

The cold sweat melted from their limbs,
Nor rot nor reek did they:
The look with which they looked on me
Had never passed away.

An orphan's curse would drag to hell
A spirit from on high;
But oh! more horrible than that
Is the curse in a dead man's eye!
Seven days, seven nights, I saw that curse,
And yet I could not die.

The moving Moon went up the sky,
And no where did abide:
Softly she was going up,
And a star or two beside—

Her beams bemocked the sultry main,
Like April hoar-frost spread;
But where the ship's huge shadow lay,
The charmed water burnt alway
A still and awful red.

Beyond the shadow of the ship,
I watched the water-snakes:
They moved in tracks of shining white,
And when they reared, the elfish light
Fell off in hoary flakes.

Within the shadow of the ship
I watched their rich attire:
Blue, glossy green, and velvet black,
They coiled and swam; and every track
Was a flash of golden fire.

O happy living things! no tongue
Their beauty might declare:
A spring of love gushed from my heart,
And I blessed them unaware:
Sure my kind saint took pity on me,
And I blessed them unaware.

The self-same moment I could pray;
And from my neck so free
The Albatross fell off, and sank
Like lead into the sea.'

PART V

'Oh sleep! it is a gentle thing,
Beloved from pole to pole!
To Mary Queen the praise be given!
She sent the gentle sleep from Heaven,
That slid into my soul.

The silly buckets on the deck,
That had so long remained,
I dreamt that they were filled with dew;
And when I awoke, it rained.

My lips were wet, my throat was cold,
My garments were all dank;
Sure I had drunken in my dreams,
And still my body drank.

I moved, and could not feel my limbs:
I was so light—almost
I thought that I had died in sleep,
And was a blessed ghost.

And soon I heard a roaring wind:
It did not come anear;
But with its sound it shook the sails,
That were so thin and sere.

The loud wind never reached the ship,
Yet now the ship moved on!
Beneath the lightning and the Moon
The dead men gave a groan.

They groaned, they stirred, they all uprose,
Nor spake, nor moved their eyes:
It had been strange, even in a dream,
To have seen those dead men rise.

The helmsman steered, the ship moved on;
Yet never a breeze up-blew;
The mariners all 'gan work the ropes,
Where they were wont to do;
They raised their limbs like lifeless tools—
We were a ghastly crew.

The body of my brother's son
Stood by me, knee to knee:
The body and I pulled at one rope,
But he said nought to me.'

'I fear thee, ancient Mariner!'
'Be calm, thou Wedding-Guest!
'Twas not those souls that fled in pain,
Which to their corses came again,
But a troop of spirits blest:

For when it dawned—they dropped their arms,
And clustered round the mast;
Sweet sounds rose slowly through their mouths,
And from their bodies passed.

Till noon we quietly sailed on,
Yet never a breeze did breathe:
Slowly and smoothly went the ship,
Moved onward from beneath.

Under the keel nine fathom deep,
From the land of mist and snow,
The spirit slid: and it was he
That made the ship to go.
The sails at noon left off their tune,
And the ship stood still also.

The Sun, right up above the mast,
Had fixed her to the ocean:
But in a minute she 'gan stir,
With a short uneasy motion—
Backwards and forwards half her length
With a short uneasy motion.

Then like a pawing horse let go,
She made a sudden bound:
It flung the blood into my head,
And I fell down in a swound.

How long in that same fit I lay,
I have not to declare;
But ere my living life returned,
I heard and in my soul discerned
Two voices in the air.

"Is it he?" quoth one, "Is this the man?
By him who died on cross,
With his cruel bow he laid full low
The harmless Albatross.

The spirit who bideth by himself
In the land of mist and snow,
He loved the bird that loved the man
Who shot him with his bow."

The other was a softer voice,
As soft as honey-dew;
Quoth he, "The man hath penance done,
And penance more will do."

PART VI
I woke and we were sailing on
As in a gentle weather:
'Twas night, calm night, the moon was high;
The dead men stood together.

All stood together on the deck,
For a charnel-dungeon fitter:
All fixed on me their stony eyes,
That in the Moon did glitter.

The pang, the curse, with which they died,
Had never passed away:
I could not draw my eyes from theirs,
Nor turn them up to pray.

But soon there breathed a wind on me,
Nor sound nor motion made:
Its path was not upon the sea,
In ripple or in shade.

It raised my hair, it fanned my cheek
Like a meadow-gale of spring—
It mingled strangely with my fears,
Yet it felt like a welcoming.

Swiftly, swiftly flew the ship,
Yet she sailed softly too:
Sweetly, sweetly blew the breeze—
On me alone it blew.

Oh! dream of joy! is this indeed
The light-house top I see?
Is this the hill? is this the kirk?
Is this mine own countree?

We drifted o'er the harbour-bar,
And I with sobs did pray—
O let me be awake, my God!
Or let me sleep alway.

The harbour-bay was clear as glass,
So smoothly it was strewn!
And on the bay the moonlight lay,
And the shadow of the Moon.

The rock shone bright, the kirk no less,
That stands above the rock:
The moonlight steeped in silentness
The steady weathercock.

And the bay was white with silent light,
Till rising from the same,
Full many shapes, that shadows were,
In crimson colours came.

A little distance from the prow
Those crimson shadows were:
I turned my eyes upon the deck—
Oh, Christ! what saw I there!

Each corse lay flat, lifeless and flat,
And, by the holy rood!
A man all light, a seraph-man,
On every corse there stood,

This seraph-band, each waved his hand:
It was a heavenly sight!
They stood as signals to the land,
Each one a lovely light;

This seraph-band, each waved his hand,
No voice did they impart—
No voice; but oh! the silence sank
Like music on my heart.

But soon I heard the dash of oars.
I heard the Pilot's cheer;
My head was turned perforce away
And I saw a boat appear.

The Pilot and the Pilot's boy,
I heard them coming fast:
Dear Lord in Heaven! it was a joy
The dead men could not blast.

I saw a third—I heard his voice:
It is the Hermit good!
He singeth loud his godly hymns
That he makes in the wood.
He'll shrieve my soul, he'll wash away
The Albatross's blood.'

PART VII
'This Hermit good lives in that wood
Which slopes down to the sea.
How loudly his sweet voice he rears!
He loves to talk with marineres
That come from a far countree.

The skiff-boat neared: I heard them talk,
"Why, this is strange, I trow!
Where are those lights so many and fair,
That signal made but now?"

"Strange, by my faith!" the Hermit said—
"And they answered not our cheer!
The planks looked warped! and see those sails,
How thin they are and sere!"

"Dear Lord! it hath a fiendish look" —
(The Pilot made reply)
"I am a-feared" —"Push on, push on!"
Said the Hermit cheerily.

The boat came closer to the ship.
But I nor spake nor stirred;
The boat came close beneath the ship,
And straight a sound was heard.

Under the water it rumbled on,
Still louder and more dread:
It reached the ship, it split the bay;
The ship went down like lead.

Stunned by that loud and dreadful sound,
Which sky and ocean smote,
Like one that hath been seven days drowned
My body lay afloat;
But swift as dreams, myself I found
Within the Pilot's boat.

Upon the whirl, where sank the ship,
The boat spun round and round;
And all was still, save that the hill
Was telling of the sound.

I moved my lips—the Pilot shrieked
And fell down in a fit;
The holy Hermit raised his eyes,
And prayed where he did sit.

I took the oars: the Pilot's boy,
Who now doth crazy go,
Laughed loud and long, and all the while
His eyes went to and fro.
"Ha! ha!" quoth he, "full plain I see
The Devil knows how to row."

And now, all in my own countree,
I stood on the firm land!
The Hermit stepped forth from the boat,
And scarcely he could stand.

"O shrieve me, shrieve me, holy man!"
The Hermit crossed his brow.
"Say quick," quoth he, "I bid thee say—
What manner of man art thou?"

Forthwith this frame of mine was wrenched
With a woful agony,
Which forced me to begin my tale;
And then it left me free.

Since then, at an uncertain hour,
That agony returns:
And till my ghastly tale is told,
This heart within me burns.

I pass, like night, from land to land;
I have strange power of speech;
That moment that his face I see,
I know the man that must hear me:
To him my tale I teach.

O Wedding-Guest! this soul hath been
Alone on a wide wide sea:
So lonely 'twas, that God himself
Scarce seemed there to be.

Farewell, farewell! but this I tell
To thee, thou Wedding-Guest!
He prayeth well, who loveth well
Both man and bird and beast.

He prayeth best, who loveth best
All things both great and small;
For the dear God who loveth us,
He made and loveth all.'

The Mariner, whose eye is bright,
Whose beard with age is hoar,
Is gone: and now the Wedding-Guest
Turned from the bridegroom's door.

He went like one that hath been stunned,
And is of sense forlorn:
A sadder and a wiser man,
He rose the morrow morn.

S T COLERIDGE (1772–1834)

A SMUGGLER'S SONG

If you wake at midnight, and hear a horse's feet,
Don't go drawing back the blind, or looking in the street.
Them that asks no questions isn't told a lie.
Watch the wall, my darling, while the Gentlemen go by!
  Five and twenty ponies,
  Trotting through the dark –
  Brandy for the Parson,
  'Baccy for the Clerk;
 Laces for a lady, letters for a spy,
And watch the wall, my darling, while the Gentlemen go by!

Running round the woodlump if you chance to find
Little barrels, roped and tarred, all full of brandy-wine,
Don't you shout to come and look, nor use 'em for your play.
Put the brushwood back again, – and they'll be gone next day!

If you see the stable-door setting open wide;
If you see a tired horse lying down inside;
If your mother mends a coat cut about and tore;
If the lining's wet and warm – don't you ask no more!

If you meet King George's men, dressed in blue and red,
You be careful what you say, and mindful what is said.
If they call you 'pretty maid', and chuck you 'neath the chin,
Don't you tell where no one is, nor yet where no one's been!

Knocks and footsteps round the house – whistles after dark –
You've no call for running out till the house-dogs bark.
Trusty's here, and *Pincher's* here, and see how dumb they lie –
They don't fret to follow when the Gentlemen go by!

If you do as you've been told, 'likely there's a chance
You'll be give a dainty doll, all the way from France,
With a cap of Valenciennes, and a velvet hood –
A present from the Gentlemen, along o' being good!
  Five and twenty ponies,
  Trotting through the dark –
  Brandy for the Parson,
  'Baccy for the Clerk;
Them that asks no questions isn't told a lie –
Watch the wall, my darling, while the Gentlemen go by!

RUDYARD KIPLING (1865–1936)

'The Ancient Mariner' is probably one of the longest poems you have come across. First, try to get to know the whole story.

In groups

- Prepare a reading of the poem, live or taped. It's probably best to tackle this as a serial in three instalments:

    Parts 1–3   journey out – killing the albatross – the spectre ship – death of the sailors.

    Parts 4–5   mariner's isolation – blessing water snakes – ghosts of sailors work the ship – Polar Spirit speeds ship to Northern waters.

    Parts 6–7   journey back – angels over the corpses of the sailors – met by the Pilot and the Hermit – ship sinks in the harbour – mariner's life of constant penance.

- Different groups could be responsible for different sections.

As a class

- Try to hear a recording of the poem on cassette or CD.
- Find a copy of *The Rime of the Ancient Mariner*, illustrated by Gustav Doré (Dover/Constable paperback). This has the full text, an outline of the events alongside the poem and 40 powerful illustrations which will help you to follow the story. (We have reproduced a few on a smaller scale here.)
- Next, map the voyage. Make a frieze or illustrated map showing the mariner's progress. Perhaps groups could work on different sections of the poem. Alongside the illustrations you could:
    — copy out suitable lines or verses from the poem;
    — invent a ship's log;
    — write the mariner's diary.

Other approaches

In groups

- There are other ways of bringing the poem alive, for example:

Movement Choose a short episode from the poem – eg the mariner's meeting with the wedding guest, killing the albatross and the changing reactions of the sailors, the dead men working the ropes – and, in groups, work out a mime or tableau to accompany the reading of the extract.

Mural A group could create a single, large picture to show the main events that happen at the three levels – air, sea, underwater. Make it a three-tiered design, perhaps with one main colour for each tier.

On your own

- *Message* Write the mariner's message in a bottle. Decide where he is (probably somewhere distant in Parts 5 or 6) and write his description of what's happened and his plea for help.

'The History of the Flood' (p. 79) lends itself to a tape-recorded reading. The nails in the Ark are heard at the beginning and end of the poem; you might have sound effects behind the first seven sections and the last four sections of the poem.

In groups

- The reading of the sections can be shared out in various ways but you might experiment with choral speaking for the nails and, in between, different individual voices for the sections on the birds, the reptiles, the insects, the fish, the raven (2), the dove (3), the coming ashore and the rainbow.

'A Smuggler's Song' (p. 95) – The smuggling of goods across the channel to the isolated villages of Devon and Cornwall was very common in years gone by and maybe something of the sort still goes on secretly today. But long ago, the smugglers were known in their villages and were often well regarded, even by the local clergy. The Excise men – King George's officers – were regarded as interfering with a long established trade and the local inhabitants did not see why they should pay the King excise duty on the goods they brought ashore. The smugglers were called the Gentlemen in the villages and if you were a child it was best you did not know who they were or what they were up to. After all, a convicted smuggler could be condemned to death.

In groups

- Prepare a reading of the poem. You could choose to have a smuggler father speaking to his daughter (which is what the title of the poem suggests) or you could choose to have a number of different smugglers' voices reading the different warning sentences and a chorus of voices reading the two repeated sections that begin 'Five and twenty ponies.' Try to maintain the steady rhythm that reminds us of the ponies' hooves throughout the poem.

'Me'

GOING THROUGH THE OLD PHOTOS

Me, my dad
and my brother
we were looking through the old photos.
Pictures of my dad with a broken leg
and my mum with big flappy shorts on
and me on a tricycle
when we got to one of my mum
with a baby on her knee,
and I go,
'Is that me or Brian?'
And my dad says,
'Let's have a look.
It isn't you or Brian,' he says.
'It's Alan.
He died.
He would have been
two years younger than Brian
and two years older than you.
He was a lovely baby.'

'How did he die?'
'Whooping cough.
I was away at the time.
He coughed himself to death in Connie's arms.
The terrible thing is,
it wouldn't happen today,
but it was during the war, you see,
and they didn't have the medicines.
That must be the only photo
of him we've got.'

Me and Brian
looked at the photo.
We couldn't say anything.
It was the first time we had ever heard about Alan.
For a moment I felt ashamed
like as if I had done something wrong.

I looked at the baby trying to work out
who he looked like.
I wanted to know what another brother
would have been like.
No way of saying.
And Mum looked so happy.
Of course she didn't know
when they took the photo
that he would die, did she?

Funny thing is,
though my father mentioned it every now and then
over the years,
Mum—never.
And he never said anything in front of her
about it
and we never let on that we knew.
What I've never figured out
was whether
her silence was because
she was more upset about it
than my dad—
or less.

MICHAEL ROSEN

CHILDHOOD

I used to think that grown-up people chose
To have stiff backs and wrinkles round their nose,
And veins like small fat snakes on either hand,
On purpose to be grand.
Till through the banisters I watched one day
My great-aunt Etty's friend who was going away,
And how her onyx beads had come unstrung.
I saw her grope to find them as they rolled;
And then I knew that she was helplessly old,
As I was helplessly young.

FRANCES CORNFORD

WATCH YOUR FRENCH

When my mum tipped a panful of red-hot fat
Over her foot, she did quite a little chat,
And I won't tell you what she said
But it wasn't:
'Fancy that!
I must try in future to be far more careful
With this red-hot scalding fat!'

When my dad fell over and landed—splat!—
With a trayful of drinks (he'd tripped over the cat)
I won't tell you what he said
But it wasn't:
'Fancy that!
I must try in future to be far more careful
To step *round* our splendid cat!'

When Uncle Joe brought me a cowboy hat
Back from the States, the dog stomped it flat,
And I won't tell you what I said
But Mum and Dad yelled:
'STOP THAT!
Where did you learn that appalling language?
Come on. Where?'
'I've no idea,' I said,
'No idea.'

KIT WRIGHT

OUT AND ABOUT, THE LADS

pants flapping round legpoles
like denim flags

necks open to the wind
their element

boots the colour of raw liver
boss the pavement

out and about
the lads

voices raised like fists
tattooed with curses

outnumbered rivals
they take in their stride

lampposts and pillarboxes
step aside

out and about
the lads

thick as thieves
and every one a star

Paul uses a knife
you dont feel a thing

Des the best speller
the aerosol king

out and about
the lads

cornered young
they will live their lives in corners

umpteenagers
out on a spree

looking for the likes
of you and me

out and about
the lads

ROGER McGOUGH

STREET BOY

Just you look at me, man,
Stompin' down the street
My crombie stuffed with biceps
My boots is filled with feet.

Just you hark to me, man,
When they call us out
My head is full of silence
My mouth is full of shout.

Just you watch me move, man,
Steady like a clock
My heart is spaced on blue beat
My soul is stoned on rock.

Just you read my name, man,
Writ for all to see
The walls is red with stories
The streets is filled with me.

GARETH OWEN

LIFE DOESN'T FRIGHTEN ME

Shadows on the wall
Noises down the hall
Life doesn't frighten me at all
Bad dogs barking loud
Big ghosts in a cloud
Life doesn't frighten me at all.

Mean old Mother Goose
Lions on the loose
They don't frighten me at all
Dragons breathing flame
On my counterpane
That doesn't frighten me at all.

I go boo
Make them shoo
I make fun
Way them run
I won't cry
So they fly
I just smile
They go wild
Life doesn't frighten me at all.

Tough guys in a fight
All alone at night
Life doesn't frighten me at all.
Panthers in the park
Strangers in the dark
No, they don't frighten me at all.

That new classroom where
Boys all pull my hair
(Kissy little girls
With their hair in curls)
They don't frighten me at all.

Don't show me frogs and snakes
And listen for my scream,
If I'm afraid at all
It's only in my dreams.

I've got a magic charm
That I keep up my sleeve,
I can walk the ocean floor
And never have to breathe.

Life doesn't frighten me at all
Not at all
Not at all
Life doesn't frighten me at all.

MAYA ANGELOU

WHO?

Who is that child I see wandering, wandering
Down by the side of the quivering stream?
Why does he seem not to hear, though I call to him?
Where does he come from, and what is his name?

Why do I see him at sunrise and sunset
Taking, in old-fashioned clothes, the same track?
Why, when he walks, does he cast not a shadow
Though the sun rises and falls at his back?

Why does the dust lie so thick on the hedgerow
By the great field where a horse pulls the plough?
Why do I see only meadows, where houses
Stand in a line by the riverside now?

Why does he move like a wraith by the water,
Soft as the thistledown on the breeze blown?
When I draw near him so that I may hear him,
Why does he say that his name is my own.

CHARLES CAUSLEY

EDEN ROCK

They are waiting for me somewhere beyond Eden Rock:
My father, twenty-five, in the same suit
Of Genuine Irish Tweed, his terrier Jack
Still two years old and trembling at his feet.

My mother, twenty-three, in a sprigged dress
Drawn at the waist, ribbon in her straw hat,
Has spread the stiff white cloth over the grass.
Her hair, the colour of wheat, takes on the light.

She pours tea from a Thermos, the milk straight
From an old H.P. sauce-bottle, a screw
Of paper for a cork; slowly sets out
The same three plates, the tin cups painted blue.

The sky whitens as if lit by three suns.
My mother shades her eyes and looks my way
Over the drifted stream. My father spins
A stone along the water. Leisurely,

They beckon to me from the other bank.
I hear them call, 'See where the stream-path is!
Crossing is not as hard as you might think.'
I had not thought that it would be like this.

CHARLES CAUSLEY

As a class

Hear Michael Rosen's poem 'Going Through the Old
Photos' (p. 98) read aloud.

- Trace the changing feelings that the poem records as the story of Alan's
  brief life is told.
- In the last section, how do different members of the family react to the
  knowledge of the baby's death and why?

On your own

- Find one or more of your own family photographs – probably with
  happier associations than Michael Rosen's – and write your own poem
  about the memories and feelings they bring back.

Performances

In pairs or groups

- Rehearse Kit Wright's poem 'Watch Your French' (3 voices) on page 100
  for presentation to the rest of the class.

Looking Back ... Looking Forward

In 'Who?' (p. 103), Charles Causley looks back and sees the ghost of
the child he once was. In 'Eden Rock' (p. 103) he recalls a childhood
incident on a family picnic which prompts him to look into the future
when he will rejoin his dead parents.

Frances Cornford's poem 'Childhood' (p. 99) also focuses on a
particular childhood memory which, in this case, altered her view of
old people. Hear the three poems read aloud.

As a class

- Talk about each of the poems in turn and make sure that you
  understand the events described.
- Explain the last two lines of each poem.

On your own

- Choose a single incident from your own early years which you
  remember because it seems to you to capture the idea of childhood, or
  a child's view of old age, or a moment when you felt you understood
  something about people older or younger than you. Tell the story of the
  incident in a few lines and then, in the last two lines, say why it is
  important to you.

Fears

At some time in our lives most of us feel very frightened. Often such fears are associated with darkness – walking home after dark, your bedroom when it's pitch black or has unfamiliar shadows; but your fears may also arise at other times and places.

As a class

● Talk about occasions when you have felt really scared. Then, hear Maya Angelou's poem 'Life Doesn't Frighten Me' (p. 102) read aloud. Talk about the fears in the poem and the ways they are overcome.

On your own

Notice how the first two verses are constructed: two rhyming lines about two fears followed by 'Life doesn't frighten me at all'. This pattern is then repeated, after which, in verse three, the fears are banished in a series of short rhyming lines.

● Write your own poem in this pattern using Maya Angelou's title and repeating it every few lines as she has done.

Gender Image

Roger McGough's 'Out and About the Lads' (p. 101) and Gareth Owen's 'Streetboy' (p. 101) are about different aspects of boys' behaviour.

In groups

● Choose *one* of the poems and decide how the reading is best shared between several voices. Rehearse your performance and present it to the rest of the class.

As a class

● Talk about the images of boys that you find in the poems. How do they differ? Is there anything in common?

On your own

● Write your own poem about a particular person or group of boys or girls which captures their behaviour. Start by deciding on your subjects and then list words and phrases to describe their clothes, ways of walking and moving, actions, speech and so on. Write up your notes into a free verse poem.

School

A BOY'S HEAD

In it there is a space-ship
and a project
for doing away with piano lessons.

And there is
Noah's ark,
which shall be first.

And there is
an entirely new bird,
an entirely new hare,
an entirely new bumble-bee.

There is a river
that flows upwards.

There is a multiplication table.

There is anti-matter.

And it just cannot be trimmed.

I believe
that only what cannot be trimmed
is a head.
There is much promise
in the circumstance
that so many people have heads.

MIROSLAV HOLUB
(trans. I. Milner and G. Theiner)

TERM BEGINS AGAIN (OSTRICH BLUES)

I find myself
in bed again
with the sheets up over
my head again

papers collect
on my desk again
reports and memos and lists again

there are the
timetables in black ink
again

the silhouetted heads
in rows against the light
again

the lists again
of books I haven't read
again

nightmares again
of assignations missed
again

of students riding off
on bicycles playing bass guitars
again

and I oversleep
again
and again

I find myself
in bed
again

with the sheets up over
my head

again

STEF PIXNER

TICH MILLER

Tich Miller wore glasses
with elastoplast-pink frames
and had one foot three sizes larger than
   the other.

When they picked teams for outdoor games
she and I were always the last two
left standing by the wire-mesh fence.

We avoided one another's eyes,
stooping, perhaps, to re-tie a shoelace,
or affecting interest in the flight

of some fortunate bird, and pretended
not to hear the urgent conference:
'Have Tubby!' 'No, no, have Tich!'

Usually they chose me, the lesser dud,
and she lolloped, unselected,
to the back of the other team.

At eleven we went to different schools.
In time I learned to get my own back,
sneering at hockey-players who couldn't spell.

Tich died when she was twelve.

WENDY COPE

OH BRING BACK HIGHER STANDARDS

Oh bring back higher standards—
the pencil and the cane—
if we want education then
   we must have some pain.
Oh, bring us back all the gone days
Yes, bring back all the past...
let's put them all in rows again—
   so we can see who's last.
Let's label all the good ones
(the ones like you and me)
and make them into prefects—
   like prefects used to be.
We'll put them on the honours board
...as honours ought to be,
and write their names
   in burnished script—
for all the world to see.
We'll have them back in uniform,
we'll have them doff their caps,
and learn what manners really are
...for decent kind of chaps!
...So let's label all the good ones,
we'll call them 'A's and 'B's—
and we'll parcel up the useless ones
and call them 'C's and 'D's.
...We'll even have an 'E' lot!
...an 'F' and 'G' maybe!!
...so they can know they're useless,
...and not as good as me.

For we've got to have the stupid—
And we've got to have the poor
Because—
         if we don't have them...
         well...what are prefects for?

PETER DIXON

Exercise Book

Two and two four
four and four eight
eight and eight sixteen...
Once again! says the master
Two and two four
four and four eight
eight and eight sixteen.
But look! the lyre bird
high on the wing
the child sees it
the child hears it
the child calls it
Save me
play with me
bird!
So the bird alights
and plays with the child
Two and two four...
Once again! says the master
and the child plays
and the bird plays too...
Four and four eight
eight and eight sixteen
and twice sixteen makes what?
Twice sixteen makes nothing
least of all thirty-two
anyhow
and off they go

For the child has hidden
The bird in his desk
and all the children
hear its song
and all the children
hear the music
and eight and eight in their turn
off they go
and four and four and two and two
in their turn fade away
and one and one make neither one nor two
but one by one off they go.
And the lyre-bird sings
and the child sings
and the master shouts
When you've quite finished playing the fool!
But all the children
Are listening to the music
And the walls of the classroom
quietly crumble.
The window panes turn
once more to sand
the ink is sea
the desk is trees
the chalk is cliffs
and the quill pen
a bird again.

PAUL DEHN

IN MRS TILSCHER'S CLASS

You could travel up the Blue Nile
with your finger, tracing the route
while Mrs Tilscher chanted the scenery.
Tana. Ethiopia. Khartoum. Aswân.
That for an hour, then a skittle of milk
and the chalky Pyramids rubbed into dust.
A window opened with a long pole.
The laugh of a bell swung by a running child.

This was better than home. Enthralling books.
The classroom glowed like a sweet shop.
Sugar paper. Coloured shapes. Brady and Hindley
faded, like the faint, uneasy smudge of a mistake.
Mrs Tilscher loved you. Some mornings, you found
she'd left a good gold star by your name.
The scent of a pencil slowly, carefully, shaved.
A xylophone's nonsense heard from another form.

Over the Easter term, the inky tadpoles changed
from commas into exclamation marks. Three frogs
hopped in the playground, freed by a dunce,
followed by a line of kids, jumping and croaking
away from the lunch queue. A rough boy
told you how you were born. You kicked him, but stared
at your parents, appalled, when you got back home.

That feverish July, the air tasted of electricity.
A tangible alarm made you always untidy, hot,
fractious under the heavy, sexy sky. You asked her
how you were born and Mrs Tilscher smiled,
then turned away. Reports were handed out.
You ran through the gates, impatient to be grown,
as the sky split open into a thunderstorm.

CAROL ANN DUFFY

THE RAILINGS

You came to watch me playing cricket once.
Quite a few of the fathers did.
At ease, outside the pavilion
they would while away a Saturday afternoon.
Joke with the masters, urge on
their flannelled offspring. But not you.

Fielding deep near the boundary
I saw you through the railings.
You were embarrassed when I waved
and moved out of sight down the road.
When it was my turn to bowl though
I knew you'd still be watching.

Third ball, a wicket, and three more followed.
When we came in at the end of the innings
the other dads applauded and joined us for tea.
Of course, you had gone by then. Later,
you said you'd found yourself there by accident.
Just passing. Spotted me through the railings.

        ★   ★   ★

Speech-days . Prize givings . School-plays
The Twentyfirst . The Wedding . The Christening
You would find yourself there by accident.
Just passing. Spotted me through the railings.

ROGER McGOUGH

Sequel

Miroslav Holub's poem, 'A Boy's Head' (p. 106), imagines some of the strange and varied things that might take up space in a boy's mind. Do you think he is right or would you suggest other items and ideas are more likely to occupy his mind? Would the things that occupy a girl's mind be the same?

On your own

- *Either* make a list of nine or ten things you think might be in a boy's head and write your own version of the poem, *or* list items that might occupy a girl's mind and write your own poem as a sequel entitled *A Girl's Head.*

Performance

'Exercise Book' by Paul Dehn (p. 108) can be read aloud in a class group.

As a class

- Hear it read aloud and discuss what you think the poem is about.
- Prepare a class reading of the poem. Decide which lines should be chanted together as a whole class and which ones need an individual voice. You may decide you need a narrator, a schoolmaster, and a child as well as the voices of the primary class reciting their tables, but other individual voices could be added by perhaps using six separate 'children's' voices to say the last six sentences.

In groups

'Oh Bring Back Higher Standards' (p. 107) seems to echo various pleas and exhortations by some politicians, some of the press and even some parents.

- Hear the poem read over once and discuss what you think the writer is suggesting. Does he mean what he seems to be saying? What do you think is his point? Do you agree with him?
- Groups could be as small as threes with the sentences each being read in turn or you could split the poem between up to nine voices with a voice for each sentence: you could even add a smug voice saying the line 'and not as good as me.'

Memories

Carol Ann Duffy remembers as a grown up fragments of her primary school days in her poem 'In Mrs Tilscher's Class' (p. 109). Although it is about primary school, it is quite a grown up poem and you may need to think about various things from birth to death in order to get to grips with it.

As a class

- Share some of your memories of being at primary school.
- Hear the poem read aloud by your teacher. Concentrate on the words and the pictures they conjure up in your mind.
  — In the first verse, what is Mrs Tilscher doing?
  — What do you think 'a skittle of milk' might be? Why is this a good description?
  — What kind of Pyramids were they and what happened to them after the break?
  — How would you describe the atmosphere of this primary classroom over 30 years ago? How did the writer feel about being in Mrs Tilscher's class?
  — Who were 'Brady and Hindley' and why, in this world, do they seem 'a mistake'?
  — Reading the last two verses together, what seems to be the main thing on the girl's mind? What prompts her?

On your own

- Jot down for about five minutes some of the impressions you retain from primary school days. What sounds, images, smells even do you remember? What voices? What games? What lessons? What was positive and comforting and what was not?
- From your jumble of ideas and impressions, see if you can begin to shape your own poem about life as you recall it in Mrs X's class or Miss Y's class or Mr Z's class: put your own primary school teacher's name in the title. Remember to concentrate on tiny details as well as on big things. Tiny details – 'The scent of a pencil carefully shaved / A xylophone's nonsense heard from another form' – are the sort of things that make us stop and say 'That's right: I remember that…'.

MACAVITY: THE MYSTERY CAT

Macavity's a Mystery Cat: he's called the Hidden Paw—
For he's the master criminal who can defy the Law.
He's the bafflement of Scotland Yard, the Flying Squad's
    despair:
For when they reach the scene of crime—*Macavity's not there!*

Macavity, Macavity, there's no one like Macavity,
He's broken every human law, he breaks the law of gravity.
His powers of levitation would make a fakir stare,
And when you reach the scene of crime—*Macavity's not
    there!*
You may seek him in the basement, you may look up in the
    air—
But I tell you once and once again, *Macavity's not there!*

Macavity's a ginger cat, he's very tall and thin;
You would know him if you saw him, for his eyes are sunken
    in.
His brow is deeply lined with thought, his head is highly
    domed;
His coat is dusty from neglect, his whiskers are uncombed.
He sways his head from side to side, with movements like a
    snake;
And when you think he's half asleep, he's always wide
    awake.

Macavity, Macavity, there's no one like Macavity,
For he's a fiend in feline shape, a monster of depravity.
You may meet him in a by-street, you may see him in the
    square—
But when a crime's discovered, then *Macavity's not there!*

He's outwardly respectable. (They say he cheats at cards.)

And his footprints are not found in any file of Scotland
  Yard's.
And when the larder's looted, or the jewel-case is rifled,
Or when the milk is missing, or another Peke's been stifled,
Or the greenhouse glass is broken, and the trellis past
  repair—
Ay, there's the wonder of the thing! *Macavity's not there!*

And when the Foreign Office find a Treaty's gone astray,
Or the Admiralty lose some plans and drawings by the way,
There may be a scrap of paper in the hall or on the stair—
But it's useless to investigate—*Macavity's not there!*
And when the loss has been disclosed, the Secret Service
  say:
'It *must* have been Macavity!'—but he's a mile away.
You'll be sure to find him resting, or a-licking of his thumbs,
Or engaged in doing complicated long division sums.

Macavity, Macavity, there's no one like Macavity,
There never was a Cat of such deceitfulness and suavity,
He always has an alibi, and one or two to spare:
At whatever time the deed took place—MACAVITY
  WASN'T THERE!
And they say that all the Cats whose wicked deeds are widely known
(I might mention Mungojerrie, I might mention Griddlebone)
Are nothing more than agents for the Cat who all the time
Just controls their operations: the Napoleon of Crime!

T S Eliot

SOLDIER FREDDY

Soldier Freddy
  was never ready,
But! Soldier Neddy,
  unlike Freddy
Was *always* ready
  and steady,

That's why,
  When Soldier Neddy
Is-outside-Buckingham-Palace-on-guard-in-the pouring-
  wind-and-rain-
    being-steady-and-ready,
  Freddy-
    is home in beddy.

Spike Milligan

HUNTER TRIALS

It's awfully bad luck on Diana,
  Her ponies have swallowed their bits;
She fished down their throats with a spanner
  And frightened them all into fits.

So now she's attempting to borrow.
  Do lend her some bits, Mummy, *do*;
I'll lend her my own for tomorrow,
  But to-day *I'll* be wanting them too.

Just look at Prunella on Guzzle;
  The wizardest pony on earth;
Why doesn't she slacken his muzzle
  And tighten the breech in his girth?

I say, Mummy, there's Mrs Geyser
  And doesn't she look pretty sick?
I bet it's because Mona Lisa
  Was hit on the hock with a brick.

Miss Blewitt says Monica threw it,
  But Monica says it was Joan,
And Joan's very thick with Miss Blewitt,
  So Monica's sulking alone.

And Margaret failed in her paces,
  Her withers got tied in a noose,
So her coronet's caught in the traces
  And now all her fetlocks are loose.

Oh, it's me now. I'm terribly nervous.
  I wonder if Smudges will shy.
She's practically certain to swerve as
  Her Pelham is over one eye.

* * *

Oh, wasn't it naughty of Smudges?
  Oh, Mummy, I'm sick with disgust.
She threw me in front of the Judges,
  And my silly old collarbone's bust.

                                     JOHN BETJEMAN

FOUR LIMERICKS

There was an old fellow of Tring
Who, when somebody asked him to sing,
  Replied, 'Ain't it odd?
  I can never tell *God*
Save the Weasel from *Pop goes the King.*'

                                     ANON

There was an old man from Darjeeling,
Who boarded a bus bound for Ealing.
  He saw on the door:
  'Please don't spit on the floor',
So he stood up and spat on the ceiling.

                                     ANON

There was an old man from Dunoon,
Who always ate soup with a fork,
  For he said, 'As I eat
  Neither fish, fowl nor flesh,
I should finish my dinner too quick.'

                                     ANON

There was a young lady called Wemyss
Who, it semyss, was troubled with dremyss.
  She would wake in the night
  And, in terrible fright,
Shake the bemyss of the house with her scremyss.

                                     ANON

THE STERN PARENT

Father heard his Children scream,
So he threw them in the stream,
Saying, as he drowned the third,
'Children should be seen, *not* heard!'

                 HARRY GRAHAM

APPRECIATION

Auntie did you feel no pain
   Falling from that willow tree?
Will you do it, please, again?
   Cos my friend here didn't see.

                 HARRY GRAHAM

UNEMPLOYABLE

'I usth thu workth in the thircusth,'
He said,
Between the intermittent showers that emerged from his
   mouth.
'Oh,' I said, 'what did you do?'
'I usth thu catcth bulleth in my theeth.'

                 GARETH OWEN

WHEN YOU'RE A GROWN-UP

When you're a GROWN-UP
a SERIOUS and SENSIBLE PERSON
When you've stopped being SILLY
you can go out and have babies
and go into a SERIOUS and SENSIBLE shop
and ask for:
Tuftytails, Paddipads, Bikkipegs, Cosytoes
and
Tommy Tippee Teethers.
Sno-bunnies, Visivents, Safeshines
Comfybaths, Dikkybibs
and
Babywipes.
Rumba Rattles and Trigger Jiggers
A Whirlee Three, a Finger Flip
or A Quacky Duck.
And if you're very SENSIBLE
you can choose
Easifitz, Baby buggies and a Safesitterstand.
Or is it a
Saferstandsit?
No it's a Sitstandsafe. I can never remember.
I'm sorry but Babytalk is a very difficult
    language
It's for adults only.
Like 'X' films
Much too horrible for children.

MICHAEL ROSEN

YOU TELL ME

Here are the football results:
League Division Fun
Manchester United won, Manchester City lost.
Crystal Palace 2, Buckingham Palace 1
Millwall Leeds nowhere
Wolves 8 A cheese roll and had a cup of tea 2
Aldershot 3 Buffalo Bill shot 2
Evertonill, Liverpool's not very well either
Newcastle's Heaven Sunderland's a very nice place 2
Ipswich one? You tell me.

MICHAEL ROSEN

Performances

Many of these poems are suitable for reading aloud, choral speaking and performing. Below are some suggestions as to how one might approach them:

T S Eliot's poem 'Macavity: The Mystery Cat' (p. 113) describes a cat who reminds us of the master criminal Moriarty who was Sherlock Holmes' arch adversary. His exploits are quite remarkable and need to be treated with the amazement they deserve.

● Prepare a reading of the poem with seven people each reading a verse and everybody joining in with 'Macavity's not there!'

'Hunter Trials' by John Betjeman (p. 115) was written many years ago but may still sound embarrassingly familiar to some. A fairly excruciating upper class accent is needed to do the poem justice.

● In pairs prepare a reading of the poem. The poem is intended for a single voice but verses 1, 2, 4, 7 and 8 can be read by one voice (mummy's little girl) and verses 3, 5 and 6 by another (her friend).

'When you're a GROWN-UP' (p. 117) can be presented using five voices.

● Voice 1 reads to line 6 'and ask for:'; Voices 2, 3 and 4 read the next three sentences up to 'A Quacky Duck'; Voice 1 returns briefly for 'And if you are very SENSIBLE you can choose' and Voice 5 continues to 'I can never remember'; Voice 1 returns to finish the poem. Apart from Voice 1 which is very sensible at all times the other voices are as silly as they can be. It is tricky getting a seamless performance but fun if you can manage it.

'You Tell Me' (p. 117) is another poem by Michael Rosen.

● You will need to think about the curious way the announcer gives the football results on radio or television if you are going to read this poem successfully. How is it that the tone of the first part of the announcement usually tells you the second part? We feel fairly sure we know the result before the announcer has finished. This poem depends upon the reader or the listener expecting one thing from the first part of each result and being surprised by an unexpected second part. Practise reading it over to yourselves and see who can give the most convincing version. It sounds best if the results are read quite seriously.

Write your own

Limericks   Everyone knows some limericks and the four on p. 115 will quickly remind you what they look like and how they work. The fourth one obstinately refuses to rhyme but you can work out for yourself what words would make it fit the pattern.

On your own

- Write your own limerick. It isn't too difficult as long as you remember that limericks usually begin with a line which mentions the subject:
  eg 'There was an old fellow of Ryde'
  or 'There was a young lad in year eight'
  or 'A teacher of maths at our school'
  — This first line rhymes with the second line and the fifth line.
  — The third and fourth lines are shorter and rhyme with each other.
  — The last line often, though not always, contains a joke. (Edward Lear, who wrote many limericks, did not end his with joke lines. He simply repeated the idea of the first line eg 'That crazy old fellow from Ryde' or 'That stupid young lad in year eight.'

  The rhythms of limericks are easy to hear, less easy to describe. It's probably best to try out your limerick on a partner and your teacher to see if there are any uneven lines that can be smoothed out.

Ruthless Rhymes is the title Harry Graham gave to his four line verses like 'Appreciation' and 'The Stern Parent' which you will find on p. 116. They have two pairs of rhyming lines (couplets) and have to be very unkind. The illustration of the Stern Parent is by Harry Graham himself.

- Compose your own Ruthless Rhyme and draw a picture to go with it.

Creatures

FIRST SIGHT

Lambs that learn to walk in snow
When their bleating clouds the air
Meet a vast unwelcome, know
Nothing but a sunless glare.
Newly stumbling to and fro
All they find, outside the fold,
Is a wretched width of cold.

As they wait beside the ewe,
Her fleeces wetly caked, there lies
Hidden round them, waiting too,
Earth's immeasurable surprise.
They could not grasp it if they knew,
What so soon will wake and grow
Utterly unlike the snow.

PHILIP LARKIN

THE SWALLOWS

All day—when early morning shone
With every dewdrop its own dawn
And when cockchafers were abroad
Hurtling like missiles that had lost their road—

The swallows twisting here and there
Round unseen corners in the air
Upstream and down so quickly passed
I wondered that their shadows flew as fast.

They steeple-chased over the bridge
And dropped down to a drowning midge
Sharing the river with the fish,
Although the air itself was their chief dish.

Blue-winged snowballs! until they turned
And then with ruddy breasts they burned;
All in one instant everywhere,
Jugglers with their own bodies in the air.

ANDREW YOUNG

WARNING TO A WORM

An alimentary tract
    undressed in flesh and bone
    should not be out alone;
that's elementary fact.

Go home, small hoover-pipe:
    go home, elastic hose
    that lacks a leg, that grows
and then contracts its shape.

Segmented, tapered tube:
    twin-ended tentacle:
    go home, small article
of food, before birds grab

and eat you. Hurry. Rush.
Beware the savage Thrush.

ANNA ADAMS

THE EAGLE

He hangs between his wings outspread
　Level and still
And bends a narrow golden head,
　Scanning the ground to kill.

Yet as he sails and smoothly swings
　Round the hill-side,
He looks as though from his own wings
　He hung down crucified.

ANDREW YOUNG

PIGEONS

They paddle with staccato feet
In powder-pools of sunlight,
Small blue busybodies
Strutting like fat gentlemen
With hands clasped
Under their swallowtail coats;
And, as they stump about,
Their heads like tiny hammers
Tap at imaginary nails
In non-existent walls.
Elusive ghosts of sunshine
Slither down the green gloss
Of their necks an instant, and are gone.

Summer hangs drugged from sky to earth
In limpid fathoms of silence:
Only warm dark dimples of sound
Slide like slow bubbles
From the contented throats.

Raise a casual hand—
With one quick gust
They fountain into air.

RICHARD KELL

THE SONG OF THE WHALE

Heaving mountain in the sea,
Whale, I heard you
Grieving.

Great whale, crying for your life,
Crying for your kind, I knew
How we would use
Your dying:

Lipstick for our painted faces,
Polish for our shoes.

Tumbling mountain in the sea,
Whale, I heard you
Calling.

Bird-high notes, keening, soaring:
At their edge a tiny drum
Like a heartbeat.
We would make you
Dumb.

In the forest of the sea,
Whale, I heard you
Singing,

Singing to your kind.
We'll never let you be.
Instead of life we choose

Lipstick for our painted faces,
Polish for our shoes.

KIT WRIGHT

THE TOM-CAT

At midnight in the alley
  A Tom-cat comes to wail,
And he chants the hate of a million years
  As he swings his snaky tail.

Malevolent, bony, brindled,
  Tiger and devil and bard,
His eyes are coals from the middle of Hell
  And his heart is black and hard.

He twists and crouches and capers
  And bares his curved sharp claws,
And he sings to the stars of the jungle nights,
  Ere cities were, or laws.

Beast from a world primeval,
  He and his leaping clan,
When the blotched red moon leers over the roofs
  Give voice to their scorn of man.

He will lie on a rug to-morrow
  And lick his silky fur,
And veil the brute in his yellow eyes
  And play he's tame and purr.

But at midnight in the alley
  He will crouch again and wail,
And beat the time for his demon's song
  With the swing of his demon's tail.

DON MARQUIS

THE BIRD-FANCIER

Up to his shoulders
In grasses coarse as silk,
The white cat with the yellow eyes
Sits with all four paws together,
Tall as a quart of milk.

He hardly moves his head
To touch with nice nose
What his wary whiskers tell him
Is here a weed
And here a rose.

On a dry stick he rubs his jaws,
And the thin
Corners of his smile
Silently mew when a leaf
Tickles his chin.

With a neat grimace
He nips a new
Blade of feathery grass,
Flicks from his ear
A grain of dew.

His sleepy eyes are wild with birds.
Every sparrow, thrush and wren
Widens their furred horizons
Till their flying song
Narrows them again.

JAMES KIRKUP

THE RABBIT

(After Prévert)
We are going to see the rabbit,
We are going to see the rabbit.
Which rabbit, people say?
Which rabbit, ask the children?
Which rabbit?
The only rabbit,
The only rabbit in England,
Sitting behind a barbed-wire fence
Under the floodlights, neon lights,
Sodium lights,
Nibbling grass
On the only patch of grass
In England, in England
(Except the grass by the hoardings
Which doesn't count.)
We are going to see the rabbit
And we must be there on time.

First we shall go by escalator,
Then we shall go by underground,
And then we shall go by motorway
And then by helicopterway,
And the last ten yards we shall have to go
On foot.

And now we are going
All the way to see the rabbit,
We are nearly there,
We are longing to see it,
And so is the crowd
Which is here in thousands

With mounted policemen
And big loudspeakers
And bands and banners,
And everyone has come a long way.
But soon we shall see it
Sitting and nibbling
The blades of grass
On the only patch of grass
In—but something has gone wrong!
Why is everyone so angry,
Why is everyone jostling
And slanging and complaining?

The rabbit has gone,
Yes, the rabbit has gone.
He has actually burrowed down into the earth
And made himself a warren, under the earth,
Despite all these people.
And what shall we do?
What *can* we do?

It is all a pity, you must be disappointed,
Go home and do something else for today,
Go home again, go home for today.
For you cannot hear the rabbit, under the earth,
Remarking rather sadly to himself, by himself,
As he rests in his warren, under the earth:
'It won't be long, they are bound to come,
They are bound to come and find me, even here.'

ALAN BROWNJOHN

Looking closely

The two poems about cats on page 122 each describe different ways of looking at these creatures. You yourself may have a cat; most of you, at one time or another, will have played with one, and you can probably suggest some reasons why people find them fascinating.

On your own/in pairs

● Write about one of the many different moods or habits of a cat: chasing a piece of string ... playing with a ball ... stalking a bird ... lapping up milk ... washing itself ... sleeping ... angry.
    Whichever of these you choose, try to capture the details of the cat's movements, sounds, appearance, and feel of its fur.

Talking and writing

Many animals are hunters. You will all have watched such everyday occurrences as a blackbird after worms, a spider ensnaring a fly, a cat stalking a bird. Some of you may have seen rarer sights – a hawk swooping on its prey, a fox after chickens, a pike darting after smaller fish.

In groups

● Discuss any incidents of this kind that you have seen. As you talk, jot down any words or phrases that seem to you to capture the *movement* of the creatures. (We have already used 'stalking', 'swooping', 'darting'.)

On your own

● Choose one incident yourself and describe in detail what you see in your mind's eye.

Performing

'The Song of the Whale' (p. 121) can be read by two or more voices with several people joining in to read the chorus lines which are printed in italics.

    'The Tom-cat' (p. 122) is another poem that can be divided up and read aloud by several different voices.

Drama

Alan Brownjohn's poem 'The Rabbit' (p. 123) can simply be split up between different voices and read aloud, but really it cries out to be acted as well. There is a main voice – maybe two or three – almost like those of parents or teachers; there is the voice of the crowd and there are the voices of the children; there is the voice of a public announcement telling people to go home and, finally, there is the small, sad voice of the rabbit. And as the story unfolds there is the journey which all the people make by escalator, underground, motorway, helicopter and on foot to where the rabbit lives. You will probably need a fairly large space to work in like a hall or drama room.

Looking and writing

Richard Kell's poem 'Pigeons' (p. 121) is full of details about how the pigeons move, what they look like, the sounds they make. All the time he is comparing the pigeons to other things – they strut 'like fat gentlemen', their heads are 'like tiny hammers' tapping 'imaginary nails'. These comparisons help us to see the picture more clearly in our mind's eye.

On your own

- Choose a creature you know well – something you can imagine clearly. It may be your pet cat or dog, a canary, goldfish, gerbil or hamster. Concentrate on its movement ... what words best describe it? What is it *like*? Concentrate on its appearance ... what words best describe it? What is it *like*? Concentrate on any sound it may make ... what words best describe it? What is it *like*?

  Jot down your ideas. Look back at what you have written. Try to shape your ideas into a poem that describes the creature you were imagining.

Seasons

handwritten notes:
- *metaphor*
- *simile*
- *personification*

FROM: SPRING NATURE NOTES

1

The sun lies mild and still on the yard stones.

The clue is a solitary daffodil – the first.

And the whole air struggling in soft excitements
Like a woman hurrying into her silks.
Birds everywhere zipping and unzipping
Changing their minds, in soft excitements,
Warming their wings and trying their voices.

The trees still spindle bare.

Beyond them, from the warmed blue hills
An exhilaration swirls upward, like a huge fish.

As under a waterfall, in the bustling pool.

Over the whole land
Spring thunders down in brilliant silence.

5

Spring bulges the hills.
The bare trees creak and shift.
Some buds have burst in tatters –
Like firework stubs.

But winter's lean bullocks
Only pretend to eat
The grass that will not come.

Then they bound like lambs, they twist in the air
They bounce their half tons of elastic
When the bale of hay breaks open.

They gambol from heap to heap,
Finally stand happy chewing their beards
Of last summer's dusty whiskers.

6
With arms swinging, a tremendous skater
On the flimsy ice of space,
The earth leans into its curve –

Thrilled to the core, some flies have waded out
An inch onto my window, to stand on the sky
And try their buzz.

> *TED HUGHES*

IN JUST-SPRING

in Just—
spring   when the world is mud—
luscious the little
lame balloonman

whistles   far   and wee

and eddieandbill come
running from marbles and
piracies and it's
spring

when the world is puddle-wonderful

the queer
old balloonman whistles
far   and   wee
and bettyandisabel come dancing

from hop-scotch and jump-rope and

it's
spring
and
        the

            goat-footed

balloonMan whistles
far
and
wee

> *E. E. CUMMINGS*

WORK AND PLAY

The swallow of summer, she toils all summer,
A blue-dark knot of glittering voltage,
A whiplash swimmer, a fish of the air.
    But the serpent of cars that crawls through the dust
    In shimmering exhaust
    Searching to slake
    Its fever in ocean
    Will play and be idle or else it will bust.

The swallow of summer, the barbed harpoon,
She flings from the furnace, a rainbow of purples,
Dips her glow in the pond and is perfect.
    But the serpent of cars that collapsed at the beach
    Disgorges its organs
    A scamper of colours
    Which roll like tomatoes
    Nude as tomatoes
    With sand in their creases
    To cringe in the sparkle of rollers and screech.

The swallow of summer, the seamstress of summer,
She scissors the blue into shapes and she sews it,
She draws a long thread and she knots it at corners.
    But the holiday people
    Are laid out like wounded
    Flat as in ovens
    Roasting and basting
    With faces of torment as space burns them blue
    Their heads are transistors
    Their teeth grit on sand grains
    Their lost kids are squalling
    While man-eating flies
    Jab electric shock needles but what can they do?

They can climb in their cars with raw bodies, raw faces
    And start up the serpent
    And headache it homeward
    A car full of squabbles
    And sobbing and stickiness
    With sand in their crannies
    Inhaling petroleum
    That pours from the foxgloves
    While the evening swallow
The swallow of summer, cartwheeling through crimson,
Touches the honey-slow river and turning
Returns to the hand stretched from under the eaves—
A boomerang of rejoicing shadow.

                                        TED HUGHES

JULY

... noon burns with its blistering breath
Around, and day dies still as death.
The busy noise of man and brute
Is on a sudden lost and mute;
Even the brook that leaps along
Seems weary of its bubbling song,
And, so soft its waters creep,
Tired silence sinks in sounder sleep.
The very flies forget to hum;
And, save the waggon rocking round,
The landscape sleeps without a sound.
The breeze is stopt, the lazy bough
Hath not a leaf that dances now;
The totter-grass upon the hill,
And spiders' threads, are standing still;
The feathers dropt from moor-hen's wing,
Which to the water's surface cling,
Are steadfast, and as heavy seem
As stones beneath them in the stream;
Hawkweed and groundsel's fanning downs
Unruffled keep their seedy crowns;
And in the oven-heated air,
Not one light thing is floating there,
Save that to the earnest eye,
The restless heat seems twittering by.

From *The Shepherd's Calendar*
JOHN CLARE (1793–1864)

AN AUTUMN MORNING

The autumn morning, waked by many a gun,
Throws o'er the fields her many-coloured light,
Wood wildly touched, close tanned, and
    stubbles dun,
A motley paradise for earth's delight;
Clouds ripple as the darkness breaks to light,
And clover plots are hid with silver mist,
One shower of cobwebs o'er the surface
    spread;
And threads of silk in strange disorder twist
Round every leaf and blossom's bottly head;
Hares in the drowning herbage scarcely steal
But on the battered pathway squat abed
And by the cart-rut nip their morning meal.
Look where we may, the scene is strange
    and new,
And every object wears a changing hue.

JOHN CLARE (1793–1864)

LEAVES

Who's killed the leaves?
>   Me, says the apple, I've killed them all.
>   Fat as a bomb or a cannonball
>   I've killed the leaves.

Who sees them drop?
>   Me, says the pear, they will leave me all bare
>   So all the people can point and stare.
>   I see them drop.

Who'll catch their blood?
>   Me, me, me, says the marrow, the marrow.
>   I'll get so rotund that they'll need a wheelbarrow.
>   I'll catch their blood.

Who'll make their shroud?
>   Me, says the swallow, there's just time enough
>   Before I must pack all my spools and be off.
>   I'll make their shroud.

Who'll dig their grave?
>   Me, says the river, with the power of the clouds
>   A brown deep grave I'll dig under my floods.
>   I'll dig their grave.

Who'll be their parson?
>   Me, says the Crow, for it is well-known
>   I study the bible right down to the bone.
>   I'll be their parson.

Who'll be chief mourner?
>   Me, says the wind, I will cry through the grass
>   The people will pale and go cold when I pass.
>   I'll be chief mourner.

Who'll carry the coffin?
>   Me, says the sunset, the whole world will weep
>   To see me lower it into the deep.
>   I'll carry the coffin.

Who'll sing a psalm?
>   Me, says the tractor, with my gear grinding glottle
>   I'll plough up the stubble and sing through my throttle.
>   I'll sing the psalm.

Who'll toll the bell?
>   Me, says the robin, my song in October
>   Will tell the still gardens the leaves are over.
>   I'll toll the bell.

TED HUGHES

SNOW IN THE SUBURBS

Every branch big with it,
Bent every twig with it;
Every fork like a white web-foot;
Every street and pavement mute:
Some flakes have lost their way, and grope back upward,
when
Meeting those meandering down they turn and descend
again.
The palings are glued together like a wall,
And there is no waft of wind with the fleecy fall.

A sparrow enters the tree,
Whereon immediately
A snow-lump thrice his own slight size
Descends on him and showers his head and eyes.
And overturns him,
And near inurns him,
And lights on a nether twig, when its brush
Starts off a volley of other lodging lumps with a rush.

The steps are a blanched slope,
Up which, with feeble hope,
A black cat comes, wide-eyed and thin;
And we take him in.

THOMAS HARDY (1840–1928)

HARD FROST

Frost called to water 'Halt!'
And crusted the moist snow with sparkling salt;
Brooks, their own bridges, stop,
And icicles in long stalactites drop,
And tench in water-holes
Lurk under gluey glass like fish in bowls.

In the hard-rutted lane
At every footstep breaks a brittle pane,
And tinkling trees ice-bound,
Changed into weeping willows, sweep the ground;
Dead boughs take root in ponds
And ferns on windows shoot their ghostly fronds.

But vainly the fierce frost
Interns poor fish, ranks trees in an armed host,
Hangs daggers from house-eaves
And on the windows ferny ambush weaves;
In the long war grown warmer
The sun will strike him dead and strip his armour.

ANDREW YOUNG

List poem

What details come to mind when you think of each of the four seasons?

On your own

● Jot down, in rough, the phrase 'Spring is ...' as the beginning of your poem. Now, try to write down *quickly* (each on a separate line) the sights, sounds, smells and activities which this season brings to mind.

   Try to make similar notes for the other three seasons. Do not spend more than three or four minutes on each: treat it like a brainstorming session.

   Use your notes as the basis for a short poem. Can your ideas be put together with those of others in the class to make a longer group poem?

Haiku

The seasons are a traditional source of inspiration for haiku poems, partly because they provide many simple, striking images.

On your own

● Write a haiku suggested by one of the following: the winter sun; winter trees; warm summer rain; first spring shoots; holly berries; fields of stubble. If you are in doubt about the haiku form look back at page 3.

Performance and Illustration

'Leaves' (p. 130) is a poem that might sound familiar. Do you recognise the patterns of questions and answers that go to make up the story?(There's a clue in the last verse).

As a class

● Read the poem aloud. A good way to do this is to have one person ask all the questions at the start of each verse and ten others to read the three-line replies of the apple, the pear, the marrow and so on.

On your own

● Each verse is a tiny word-picture – a bit like a haiku – only here the pictures are put together to tell an autumn story about the death and funeral of the leaves. Illustrate the poem either by
  (a) drawing and colouring a series of ten pictures, one for each verse, which can be put up as a wall display; or by
  (b) designing one large picture, perhaps a poster, which includes each of the things mentioned in the ten verses. Think carefully about the layout. Which figure is the most important? Is it better to make your picture tall and thin to catch the fall of the leaves from the tree to the grave, or to place the objects in a wide landscape?

Try to include as many of the words of the poem as possible in your illustration.

Phrase Collage

In this section, each of the four seasons is represented by two poems.

In groups/in pairs

● Choose *one* season and read the poems about it carefully. Then, write down the phrases from the poems that seem to you to capture the idea of that season. Arrange these phrases as a collage of quotations. Give your collage a title and perhaps add some seasonal illustrations.

Magic and Mystery

THE WAY THROUGH THE WOODS

They shut the road through the woods
Seventy years ago.
Weather and rain have undone it again,
And now you would never know
There was once a road through the woods
Before they planted the trees.
It is underneath the coppice and heath
And the thin anemones.
Only the keeper sees
That, where the ring-dove broods,
And the badgers roll at ease,
There was once a road through the woods.

Yet, if you enter the woods
Of a summer evening late,
When the night-air cools on the trout-ringed pools
Where the otter whistles his mate,
(They fear not men in the woods,
Because they see so few)
You will hear the beat of a horse's feet,
And the swish of a skirt in the dew,
Steadily cantering through
The misty solitudes,
As though they perfectly knew
The old lost road through the woods...
But there is no road through the woods.

RUDYARD KIPLING (1865–1936)

THE MAGIC WOOD

The wood is full of shining eyes,
The wood is full of creeping feet,
The wood is full of tiny cries:
You must not go to the wood at night!

I met a man with eyes of glass
And a finger as curled as the wriggling worm,
And hair all red with rotting leaves,
And a stick that hissed like a summer snake.

The wood is full of shining eyes,
The wood is full of creeping feet,
The wood is full of tiny cries:
You must not go to the wood at night!

He sang me a song in backwards words,
And drew me a dragon in the air.
I saw his teeth through the back of his head,
And a rat's eyes winking from his hair.

The wood is full of shining eyes,
The wood is full of creeping feet,
The wood is full of tiny cries:
You must not go to the wood at night!

He made me a penny out of a stone,
And showed me the way to catch a lark
With a straw and a nut and a whispered word
And a pennorth of ginger wrapped up in a leaf.

The wood is full of shining eyes,
The wood is full of creeping feet,
The wood is full of tiny cries:
You must not go to the wood at night!

He asked me my name, and where I lived:
I told him a name from my Book of Tales;
He asked me to come with him into the wood
And dance with the Kings from under the hills.

The wood is full of shining eyes,
The wood is full of creeping feet,
The wood is full of tiny cries:
You must not go to the wood at night!

But I saw that his eyes were turning to fire;
I watched the nails grow on his wriggling hand;
And I said my prayers, all out in a rush,
And found myself safe on my father's land.

Oh, the wood is full of shining eyes,
The wood is full of creeping feet,
The wood is full of tiny cries:
You must not go to the wood at night!

HENRY TREECE

THE GARDEN SEAT

Its former green is blue and thin,
And its once firm legs sink in and in;
Soon it will break down unaware,
Soon it will break down unaware.

At night when reddest flowers are black,
Those who once sat thereon come back;
Quite a row of them sitting there,
Quite a row of them sitting there.

With them the seat does not break down,
Nor winter freeze them, nor floods drown,
For they are as light as upper air,
They are as light as upper air!

THOMAS HARDY (1840–1928)

GHOSTS

That's right. Sit down and talk to me.
What do you want to talk about?

Ghosts. You were saying that you believe in them.
Yes, they exist, without a doubt.

What, bony white nightmares that rattle and glow?
No, just spirits that come and go.

I've never heard such a load of rubbish.
Never mind, one day you'll know.

What makes you so sure?

I said:
What makes you so sure?

Hey,
Where did you go?

KIT WRIGHT

HIST WHIST

hist   whist
little ghostthings
tip-toe
twinkle-toe

little twitchy
witches and tingling
goblins
hob-a-nob   hob-a-nob

little hoppy happy
toad in tweeds
tweeds
little itchy mousies

with scuttling
eyes   rustle and run   and
hidehidehide
whisk

whisk   look out for the old woman
with the wart on her nose
what she'll do to yer
nobody knows

for she knows the devil   ooch
the devil   ouch
the devil
ach   the great

green
dancing
devil
devil

devil
devil

    wheeEEE

E. E. Cummings

FLANNAN ISLE

'Though three men dwell on Flannan Isle
To keep the lamp alight,
As we steer'd under the lee, we caught
No glimmer through the night.'

A passing ship at dawn had brought
The news; and quickly we set sail,
To find out what strange thing might ail
The keepers of the deep-sea light.

The winter day broke blue and bright,
With glancing sun and glancing spray,
As o'er the swell our boat made way,
As gallant as a gull in flight.

But, as we near'd the lonely Isle,
And looked up at the naked height;
And saw the lighthouse towering white,
With blinded lantern, that all night
Had never shot a spark
Of comfort through the dark,
So ghostly in the cold sunlight
It seem'd, that we were struck the while
With wonder all too deep for words.

And, as into the tiny creek
We stole beneath the hanging crag,
We saw three queer, black, ugly birds—
Too big, by far, in my belief,
For guillemot or shag—
Like seamen sitting bolt-upright
Upon a half-tide reef:
But, as we near'd, they plunged from sight,
Without a sound, or spurt of white.

And still too mazed to speak,
We landed; and made fast the boat;
And climb'd the track in single file,
Each wishing he was safe afloat,
On any sea, however, far,
So it be far from Flannan Isle:
And still we seem'd to climb, and climb,
As though we'd lost all count of time,
And so must climb for evermore.

Yet, all too soon, we reached the door—
The black, sun-blister'd lighthouse-door,
That gaped for us ajar.

As, on the threshold, for a spell,
We paused, we seem'd to breathe the smell
Of limewash and of tar,
Familiar as our daily breath,
As though 'twere some strange scent of death:
And so, yet wondering, side by side,
We stood a moment, still tongue-tied:
And each with black foreboding eyed
The door, ere we should fling it wide,
To leave the sunlight for the gloom:
Till, plucking courage up, at last,
Hard on each other's heels we pass'd
Into the living-room.

Yet, as we crowded through the door,
We only saw a table, spread
For dinner, meat and cheese and bread;
But all untouch'd; and no one there:
As though, when they sat down to eat,
Ere they could even taste,
Alarm had come; and they in haste
Had risen and left the bread and meat:
For at the table-head a chair
Lay tumbled on the floor.
We listen'd; but we only heard
The feeble chirping of a bird
That starved upon its perch:
And, listening still, without a word,
We set about our hopeless search.

We hunted high, we hunted low,
And soon ransack'd the empty house;
Then o'er the Island, to and fro,
We ranged, to listen and to look
In every cranny, cleft or nook
That might have hid a bird or mouse:
But, though we search'd from shore to shore,
We found no sign in any place:
And soon again stood face to face
Before the gaping door:
And stole into the room once more
As frighten'd children steal.

Aye: though we hunted high and low,
And hunted everywhere,
Of the three men's fate we found no trace
Of any kind in any place,
But a door ajar, and an untouch'd meal,
And an overtoppled chair.

And, as we listen'd in the gloom
Of that forsaken living-room—
A chill clutch on our breath—
We thought how ill-chance came to all
Who kept the Flannan Light;
And how the rock had been the death
Of many a likely lad:
How six had come to a sudden end,
And three had gone stark mad:
And one whom we'd all known as friend

Had leapt from the lantern one still night,
And fallen dead by the lighthouse wall:
And long we thought
On the three we sought,
And of what might yet befall.

Like curs a glance has brought to heel,
We listen'd, flinching there:
And look'd, and look'd, on the untouch'd meal
And the overtoppled chair.

We seem'd to stand for an endless while,
Though still no word was said,
Three men alive on Flannan Isle,
Who thought on three men dead.

WILFRID WILSON GIBSON

KUBLA KHAN

In Xanadu did Kubla Khan
A stately pleasure-dome decree:
Where Alph, the sacred river, ran
Through caverns measureless to man
   Down to a sunless sea.
So twice five miles of fertile ground
With walls and towers were girdled round:
And there were gardens bright with sinuous rills,
Where blossomed many an incense-bearing tree;
And here were forests ancient as the hills,
Enfolding sunny spots of greenery.
But oh! that deep romantic chasm which slanted
Down the green hill athwart a cedarn cover!
A savage place! as holy and enchanted
As e'er beneath a waning moon was haunted
By woman wailing for her demon-lover!
And from this chasm, with ceaseless turmoil seething,
As if this earth in fast thick pants were breathing,
A mighty fountain momently was forced:
Amid whose swift half-intermitted burst
Huge fragments vaulted like rebounding hail,
Or chaffy grain beneath the thresher's flail:
And 'mid these dancing rocks at once and ever
It flung up momently the sacred river.
Five miles meandering with a mazy motion
Through wood and dale the sacred river ran,

Then reached the caverns measureless to man,
And sank in tumult to a lifeless ocean:
And 'mid this tumult Kubla heard from far
Ancestral voices prophesying war!

The shadow of the dome of pleasure
Floated midway on the waves;
Where was heard the mingled measure
From the fountain and the caves.
It was a miracle of rare device,
A sunny pleasure-dome with caves of ice!

A damsel with a dulcimer
In a vision once I saw:
It was an Abyssinian maid,
And on her dulcimer she played,
Singing of Mount Abora.
Could I revive within me
Her symphony and song,
To such a deep delight 'twould win me,
That with music loud and long,
I would build that dome in air,
That sunny dome! Those caves of ice!
And all who heard should see them there,
And all should cry, Beware! Beware!
His flashing eyes, his floating hair!
Weave a circle round him thrice,
And close your eyes with holy dread,
For he on honey-dew hath fed,
And drunk the milk of Paradise.

S T COLERIDGE (1772–1834)

Performing

Kit Wright's 'Ghosts' (p. 136) is written as a ghostly conversation, and can be performed by two voices. It needs careful rehearsal (use a tape-recorder to practise) and experiment with getting the right ghostly tones.

'The Magic Wood' by Henry Treece (p. 134–135) can make a powerful performance – you might choose to work on it in a drama room rather than a classroom – and can involve a large group. The hypnotic, chanted chorus can be said by the whole class or different groups of about five people can say the lines each time they appear. The main story can be given to one voice and two other people can act it out in a mime.

'Hist whist' (p. 137) can be spoken by three voices, alternating solo, duet and trio, to create light, quick, witchy sounds.

Detectives

Listen to 'Flannan Isle' (pp. 138–139) read aloud.

In groups

- Re-read and talk about the poem and make a list of the evidence for the disappearance of the three men. Note down any clues, however small, about the position and size of the lighthouse, its history, the time of year, the atmosphere of the place, what the visitors found... What do *you* think happened? Each group can present a brief report to the rest of the class, outlining its solution to the mystery.

In a class

- Hear the poem read aloud again and try to decide whose explanation is the most likely one.

Inside The Pleasure Dome

The full title of Coleridge's poem on pp. 139–140 is 'Kubla Khan: a Vision in a Dream'. The story of how it came to be written is well-known: Coleridge took opium and fell asleep while reading about the Khan (a prince or ruler) Kubla and the palace he commanded to be built. When he woke up he was aware of having composed two or three hundred lines on this theme in his head and he quickly began to write them down. Unfortunately, he was then interrupted by 'a person from Porlock', a nearby village, and when he returned to his task he had forgotten all but this fragment of 54 lines. What we are left with is 'a vision in a dream' or, rather a series of vivid word-pictures, typical of the way dreams develop without any logical story.

- Hear the poem read aloud. It falls into two parts: the first 36 lines describe an enclosed park with the palace or 'stately pleasure dome' at its centre; the remaining lines, beginning 'A damsel with a dulcimer', give another vision where the poet claims that he can build a finer, more magical dome than Kubla's.

In pairs

- Talk about the geography of the landscape in the opening part.
- Find the lines in the poem that describe the following details of the dream and talk about the pictures they create in your mind's eye:

  — *the subterranean river Alph* which bursts from a chasm in a 'mighty fountain', the caverns on its course, and the 'sunless sea' into which it flows;
  — *the landscape* around this 'sacred river' with its walled gardens and ancient forests;
  — *the dome itself* rising above this artificial paradise, ten miles in diameter, which casts its shadow on the water.

- Now, draw a map of the area, perhaps with small inset pictures of the main details and phrases from the poem as captions.

On your own/in pairs

- Describe your own imaginary dream landscape in verse; or, tongue-in-cheek, imitate Coleridge's style and write about the Millenium Dome: 'On Greenwich shore did...'! Carry on.

PART C

Ten Poets

GEOFFREY CHAUCER, *c.1343–1400*

Geoffrey Chaucer was the son of a well-to-do London wine merchant and had plenty of opportunities during his childhood to mix with all sorts of people in trade and commerce. In his early teens he became a page boy in the household of one of King Edward III's sons and, during the rest of his life, he continued to work as a courtier, civil servant, and diplomat for three successive kings: Edward III, Richard II and Henry IV who came to the throne the year before Chaucer died.

Chaucer's work kept him busy: he travelled abroad as a soldier and on affairs of state, mostly to France and Italy. He became a JP and a Knight of the Shire (Member of Parliament) for the county of Kent. For 12 years he was controller of the Customs and subsidies in the port of London for England's largest trade – the wool trade; and, later in life, he held posts as varied as Clerk of the King's Works and Deputy Forester of an area of Somerset owned by the Crown. Throughout his career he was meeting people from all walks of life and these experiences, along with the knowledge he gained from his studies, helped to shape the characters and stories that go to make up his greatest work – 'The Canterbury Tales', written during the last 15 years of his life.

The Canterbury Tales

The Journey, the Story-tellers and their Tales
'The Canterbury Tales' is a collection of 24 stories of different kinds told by members of a company of Pilgrims on a journey one Spring from the Tabard Inn in Southwark, South London to the shrine of Thomas à Becket at Canterbury in Kent.

Before the tales, Chaucer gives us a General Prologue in which he describes the appearance, character and occupation of 22 of the pilgrims – the other seven are just listed. The overall idea is outlined by Harry Bailey, the Host, when the company is gathered in the Tabard on the evening before departure. It is this: to make their journey more entertaining, each pilgrim shall tell four stories (two on the way to Canterbury, two on the way back); and the prize for the best story-teller is a free dinner at the Tabard. It was an ambitious plan: with Chaucer himself joining in as a story-teller, the company of 30 travellers was supposed to tell (and listen to) 120 stories! It is not surprising that it remained unfinished; nonetheless, these two dozen tales are the greatest single collection in the language.

Throughout the story-telling, we are often reminded of the journey and the audience. Chaucer mentions the towns the travellers visit on the way to Canterbury; their route takes them via Deptford, Greenwich, Rochester and Sittingbourne. He also writes in links between the tales, ranging from respectful comments to violent rows between the tellers and listeners. Harry Bailey, the Host, has a lot to say during these interludes.

Map of *The Pilgrim's Way* – Southwark to Canterbury

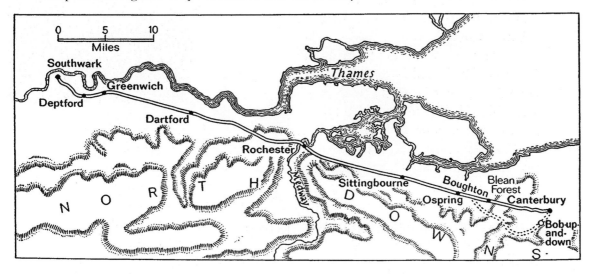

One of the main attractions of 'The Canterbury Tales' is the variety of tellers as well as of their stories. There is a wide range of characters of whom we introduce you to just three – the Miller, the Wife of Bath and the Pardoner. The two men are rogues and the Wife of Bath is a very worldly women who tells us with some relish that she has had five husbands. They, like their companions, tell stories appropriate to their personality and station in life. In the selections that follow, there are the opening and closing passages of 'The General Prologue' which set up the story-telling plan, together with the pen-portraits of these three pilgrims. This is followed by a self-contained extract – a story within a story – from 'The Pardoner's Tale'.

The Miller ▲   ▲ *The Wife of Bath*

William Blake, 'The Canterbury Pilgrims', 1810.

Speaking the lines

Remember – these are stories in verse which were supposed to be spoken aloud to entertain the company. So, why not have a go yourself at speaking Chaucer? The easiest way is to listen to a tape recording of the passages we have printed, following in the text, and then try to imitate the sounds. (Recommended recording: 'The Prologue and The Pardoner's Tale' read in Middle English, Argo (2 cassettes) SAY 24).

Here are some rules of thumb to get you started:

Vowel sounds	i)	the final -e or -es of words is spoken as an extra syllable.
	ii)	doubling the vowel -ee, -oo, -aa usually lengthens the sound.
	iii)	-a is pronounced flat, as in Northern English.

▲ *The Pardoner*

Consonant sounds: all consonants are pronounced, eg:

    i) 'Knyght' – the initial 'k' plus 'gh' as in 'loch',
        and the final 't'.
    ii) 'folk' – pronounce the 'l'
    iii) 'ion' or 'ious' – pronounce in two syllables.

Don't be afraid of making mistakes. Once you get used to the sounds
and rhythm of the lines, you will find that the characters and stories
are more colourful in Chaucer's language than in the modern version
alongside. We have provided this recent translation to help you with
difficult words and to give continuity to the descriptions and to 'The
Pardoner's Tale', but don't let it stop you speaking Chaucer's lines.
To read that the Miller had a tuft of hairs on a wart on the end of his
nose sounds rather tame beside:

'Upon the cop right of his nose he hade
A werte, and theron stood a toft of herys,
Reed as the brustles of a sowes erys . . .'

FROM: THE GENERAL PROLOGUE

(1) The Introduction

The Prologue begins with an 18-line sentence in praise of Spring and
an explanation of the company gathered at the Tabard Inn.

PROLOGUE

Whan that Aprill with his shoures soote
The droghte of March hath perced to the
  roote,
And bathed every veyne in swich licour
Of which vertu engendred is the flour;
Whan Zephirus eek with his sweete breeth
Inspired hath in every holt and heeth
The tendre croppes, and the yonge sonne
Hath in the Ram his halve cours yronne,
And smale foweles maken melodye,
That slepen al the nyght with open ye
(So priketh hem nature in hir corages);
Thanne longen folk to goon on pilgrimages,
And palmeres for to seken straunge strondes,
To ferne halwes, kowthe in sondry londes;
And specially from every shires ende
Of Engelond to Caunterbury they wende,
The hooly blisful martir for to seke,
That hem hath holpen whan that they were
  seeke.
    Bifil that in that seson on a day,
In Southwerk at the Tabard as I lay
Redy to wenden on my pilgrymage
To Caunterbury with ful devout corage,
At nyght was come into that hostelrye
Wel nyne and twenty in a compaignye,
Of sondry folk, by aventure yfalle
In felaweshipe, and pilgrimes were they alle,
That toward Caunterbury wolden ryde.
The chambres and the stables weren wyde,
And wel we weren esed atte beste.
And shortly, whan the sonne was to reste,
So hadde I spoken with hem everichon
That I was of hir felaweship anon,
And made forward erly for to rise,
To take oure wey there as I yow devyse.

---

[1] 1st sign of the Zodiac
[2] pilgrims who had visited Jerusalem
[3] St Thomas à Becket

TRANSLATION

When the sweet showers of April have
  pierced
The drought of March, and pierced it to the
  root,
And every vein is bathed in that moisture
Whose quickening force will engender the
  flower;
And when the west wind too with its sweet
  breath
Has given life in every wood and field
To tender shoots, and when the struggling
  sun
Has run his half-course in Aries, the Ram[1],
And when small birds are making melodies,
That sleep all the night long with open eyes,
(Nature so prompts them, and encourages);
Then people long to go on pilgrimages,
And palmers[2] to take ship for foreign shores,
And distant shrines, famous in different lands;
And most especially, from all the shires
Of England, to Canterbury they come
The holy blessed martyr[3] there to seek,
Who gave his help to them when they were
  sick.
    It happened at this season, that one day
In Southwark at the Tabard where I stayed
Ready to set out on my pilgrimage
To Canterbury, and pay devout homage,
There came at nightfall to the hostelry
Some nine-and-twenty in a company,
Folk of all kinds, met in accidental
Companionship, for they were pilgrims all;
It was to Canterbury that they rode.
The bedrooms and the stables were good-
  sized,
The comforts offered us were of the best.
And by the time the sun had gone to rest
I'd talked with everyone, and soon became
One of their company, and promised them
To rise at dawn next day to take the road
For the journey I am telling you about.

(2) Three Characters

THE MILLER

The MILLERE was a stout carl for the nones;
Ful byg he was of brawn, and eek of bones.
That proved wel, for over al ther he cam,
At wrastlynge he wolde have alwey the ram.
He was short-sholdred, brood, a thikke
  knarre;
Ther was no dore that he nolde heve of
  harre,
Or breke it at a rennyng with his heed.
His berd as any sowe or fox was reed,
And therto brood, as thought it were a spade.
Upon the cop right of his nose he hade
A werte, and theron stood a toft of herys,
Reed as the brustles of a sowes erys;
His nosethirles blake were and wyde.
A swerd and bokeler bar he by his syde.
His mouth as greet was as a greet forneys.
He was a janglere and a goliardeys.
And that was moost of synne and harlotries.
Wel koude he stelen corn and tollen thries;
And yet he hadde a thombe of gold, pardee.
A whit cote and a blew hood wered he.
A baggepipe wel koude he blowe and sowne,
And therwithal he broghte us out of towne.

The miller was a burly fellow—brawn
And muscle, big of bones as well as strong
As was well seen—he always won the ram
At wrestling-matches up and down the land.
He was barrel-chested, rugged and thickset,
And would heave off its hinges any door
Or break it running at it with his head.
His beard was red as any fox or sow,
And wide at that, as though it were a spade.
And on his nose, right on its tip, he had
A wart, upon which stood a tuft of hairs
Red as the bristles are in a sow's ear.
Black were his nostrils; black and squat and
  wide.
He bore a sword and buckler by his side.
His big mouth was as big as a furnace.
A loudmouth and a teller of blue stories
(Most of them vicious or scurrilous),
Well versed in stealing corn and trebling
  dues,
He had a golden thumb—by God he had!
A white coat he had on, and a blue hood.
He played the bagpipes well, and blew a tune,
And to its music brought us out of town.

The Miller

The Wife of Bath

THE WIFE OF BATH

A good WIF was ther OF biside BATHE,
But she was somdel deef, and that was scathe.
Of clooth-makyng she hadde swich an haunt,
She passed hem of Ypres and of Gaunt.
In al the parisshe wif ne was ther noon
That to the offrynge bifore hire sholde goon;
And if ther dide, certeyn so wrooth was she,
That she was out of alle charitee.
Hir coverchiefs ful fyne weren of ground;
I dorste swere they weyeden ten pound
That on a Sonday weren upon hir heed.
Hir hosen weren of fyn scarlet reed,
Ful streite yteyd, and shoes ful moyste and
  newe.
Boold was hir face, and fair, and reed of
  hewe.
She was a worthy womman al hir lyve:
Housbondes at chirche dore she hadde fyve,
Withouten oother compaignye in youthe,—
But therof nedeth nat to speke as nowthe.
And thries hadde she been at Jerusalem;
She hadde passed many a straunge strem;
At Rome she hadde been, and at Boloigne,
In Galice at Seint-Jame, and at Coloigne.
She koude muchel of wandrynge by the
  weye.
Gat-tothed was she, soothly for to seye.
Upon an amblere esily she sat,
Ywympled wel, and on hir heed an hat
As brood as is a bokeler or a targe;
A foot-mantel aboute hir hipes large,
And on hir feet a paire of spores sharpe.
In felawshipe wel koude she laughe and
  carpe.
Of remedies of love she knew per chaunce,
For she koude of that art the olde daunce.

There was a business woman, from near
  Bath,
But, more's the pity, she was a bit deaf;
So skilled a clothmaker, that she outdistanced
Even the weavers of Ypres and Ghent.
In the whole parish there was not a woman
Who dared precede her at the almsgiving,
And if there did, so furious was she,
That she was put out of all charity.
Her headkerchiefs were of the finest weave,
Ten pounds and more they weighed, I do
  believe,
Those that she wore on Sundays on her head.
Her stockings were of finest scarlet red,
Very tightly laced; shoes pliable and new.
Bold was her face, and handsome; florid too.
She had been respectable all her life,
And five times married, that's to say in
  church,
Not counting other loves she'd had in youth,
Of whom, just now, there is no need to speak.
And she had thrice been to Jerusalem;
Had wandered over many a foreign stream;
And she had been at Rome, and at Boulogne,
St James of Compostella, and at Cologne;
She knew all about wandering—and straying:
For she was gap-toothed, if you take my
  meaning[1].
Comfortably on an ambling horse she sat,
Well-wimpled, wearing on her head a hat
That might have been a shield in size and
  shape;
A riding-skirt round her enormous hips,
Also a pair of sharp spurs on her feet.
In company, how she could laugh and joke!
No doubt she knew of all the cures for love,
For at that game she was a past mistress.

---

[1]   a sign of sensuality

THE PARDONER

This PARDONER hadde heer as yelow as wex,
But smothe it heeng as dooth a strike of flex;
By ounces henge his lokkes that he hadde,
And therwith he his shuldres overspradde;
But thynne it lay, by colpons oon and oon.
But hood, for jolitee, wered he noon,
For it was trussed up in his walet.
Hym thoughte he rood al of the newe jet;
Dischevelee, save his cappe, he rood al bare.
Swiche glarynge eyen hadde he as an hare.
A vernycle hadde he sowed upon his cappe.
His walet lay biforn hym in his lappe,
Bretful of pardoun, comen from Rome al
  hoot.
A voys he hadde as smal as hath a goot.
No berd hadde he, ne nevere sholde have;
As smothe it was as it were late shave.
I trowe he were a geldyng or a mare.
But of his craft, fro Berwyk into Ware,
Ne was ther swich another pardoner.
For in his male he hadde a pilwe-beer,
Which that he seyde was Oure Lady veyl;
He seyde he hadde a gobet of the seyl
That Seint Peter hadde, whan that he wente
Upon the see, til Jhesu Crist hym hente.
He hadde a croys of latoun ful of stones,
And in a glas he hadde pigges bones.
But with thise relikes, whan that he fond
A povre person dwellynge upon londe,
Upon a day he gat hym moore moneye
Than that the person gat in monthes tweye;
And thus, with feyned flaterye and japes,
He made the person and the peple his apes.
But trewely to tellen atte laste,
He was in chirche a noble ecclesiaste.
Wel koude he rede a lessoun or a storie,
But alderbest he song an offertorie;
For wel he wiste, whan that song was songe,
He moste preche and wel affile his tonge
To wynne silver, as he ful wel koude;
Therefore he song the murierly and loude.

This pardon-seller's hair was yellow as wax,
And sleekly-hanging, like a hank of flax.
In meagre clusters hung what hair he had;
Over his shoulders a few strands were spread,
But they lay thin, in rat's tails, one by one.
As for a hood, for comfort he wore none,
For it was stowed away in his knapsack.
Save for a cap, he rode with head all bare,
Hair loose; he thought it was the *dernier cri*.
He had big bulging eyes, just like a hare.
He'd sewn a veronica[1] on his cap.
His knapsack lay before him, on his lap.
Chockful of pardons, all come hot from
  Rome.
His voice was like a goat's, plaintive and thin.
He had no beard, nor was he like to have;
Smooth was his face, as if he had just shaved.
I took him for a gelding or a mare.
As for his trade, from Berwick down to Ware
You'd not find such another pardon-seller.
For in his bag he had a pillowcase
Which had been, so he said, Our Lady's veil;
He said he had a snippet of the sail
St Peter had, that time he walked upon
The sea, and Jesus Christ caught hold of him.
And he'd a brass cross, set with pebble-stones,
And a glass reliquary of pigs' bones.
But with these relics, when he came upon
Some poor up-country priest or backwoods
  parson,
In just one day he'd pick up far more money
Than any parish priest was like to see
In two whole months. With double-talk and
  tricks
He made the people and the priest his dupes.
But to speak the truth and do the fellow
  justice,
In church he made a splendid ecclesiastic.
He'd read a lesson, or saint's history,
But best of all he sang the offertory:
For, knowing well that when the hymn was
  sung,
He'd have to preach and polish and smooth
  his tongue
To raise—as only he knew how—the wind,
The louder and the merrier he would sing.

---

[1] a copy of the handkerchief of St Veronica

(3) The Story-telling Plan

At the end of the Prologue, Chaucer as one of the company, explains
his role as the story-teller of this Pilgrimage and covers himself from
any criticism that might come his way because of the stories he tells
and the language he uses.

   Now have I toold you soothly, in a clause,
Th'estaat, th'array, the nombre and eek the
   cause
Why that assembled was this compaignye
In Southwerk at this gentil hostelrye
That highte the Tabard, faste by the Belle.
But now is tyme to yow for to telle
How that we baren us that ilke nyght,
Whan we were in that hostelrie alyght;
And after wol I telle of our viage
And al the remenaunt of our pilgrimage.
But first I pray yow, of youre curteisye,
That ye n'arette it nat my vileynye,
Thogh that I pleynly speke in this mateere,
To telle yow hir wordes and hir cheere,
Ne thogh I speke hir wordes proprely.
For this ye knowen al so wel as I,
Whoso shal telle a tale after a man,
He moot reherce as ny as evere he kan
Everich a word, if it be in his charge,
Al speke he never so rudeliche and large,
Or ellis he moot telle his tale untrewe,
Or feyne thyng, or fynde wordes newe.

   And now I've told you truly and concisely
The rank, and dress, and number of us all,
And why we gathered in a company
In Southwark, at that noble hostelry
Known as the Tabard, that's hard by the Bell.
But now the time has come for me to tell
What passed among us, what was said and
   done
That night of our arrival at the inn;
And afterwards I'll tell you how we
   journeyed,
And all the remainder of our pilgrimage.
But first I beg you, not to put it down
To my ill-breeding, if my speech be plain
When telling what they looked like, what
   they said.
Or if I use the exact words they used.
For, as you all must know as well as I,
To tell a tale told by another man
You must repeat as nearly as you can
Each word, if that's the task you've
   undertaken,
However coarse or broad his language is;
Or, in the telling, you'll have to distort it
Or make things up, or find new words for it.
You can't hold back, even if he's your brother:
Whatever word is used, you must use also.

The host, Harry Bailey, describes the Story-telling plan.

'Lordynges,' quod he, 'now herkneth for the
  beste;
But taak it nought, I prey yow, in desdeyn.
This is the poynt, to speken short and pleyn,
That ech of yow, to shorte with oure weye,
In this viage shal telle tales tweye
To Caunterbury-ward, I mene it so,
And homward he shal tellen othere two,
Of aventures that whilom han bifalle.
And which of yow that bereth hym best of
  alle,
That is to seyn, that telleth in this caas
Tales of best sentence and moost solaas,
Shal have a soper at oure aller cost
Heere in this place, sittynge by this post,
Whan that we come agayn fro Caunterbury.
And for to make yow the moore mury,
I wol myselven goodly with yow ryde,
Right at myn owene cost, and be youre gyde;
And whoso wole my juggement withseye
Shal paye al that we spenden by the weye.
And if ye vouche sauf that it be so,
Tel me anon, withouten wordes mo,
And I wol erly shape me therfore.'

'Ladies and gentlemen,' began our host,
'Do yourselves a good turn, and hear me out:
But please don't turn your noses up at it.
I'll put it in a nutshell: here's the nub:
It's that you each, to shorten the long journey,
Shall tell two tales *en route* to Canterbury,
And, coming homeward, tell another two,
Stories of things that happened long ago.
Whoever best acquits himself, and tells
The most amusing and instructive tale,
Shall have a dinner, paid for by us all,
Here in this inn, and under this roof-tree,
When we come back again from Canterbury.
To make it the more fun, I'll gladly ride
With you at my own cost, and be your guide.
And anyone who disputes what I say
Must pay all our expenses on the way!
And if this plan appeals to all of you,
Tell me at once, and with no more ado,
And I'll make my arrangements here and
  now.'

The Pardoner's Tale

Pardoners were minor Church officers whose job it was – with the
supposed authority of the Pope – to sell divine forgiveness for cash.
Chaucer's Pardoner, as we have seen from this mocking pen-portrait, is a
particularly unpleasant man. He is a smooth talker who cheats the poor and
ignorant into parting with their money to buy phoney relics which, he tells
them, will save them from punishment for their sins.

Telling a good tale is essential to this Pardoner's job as a religious
confidence trickster. So, before the story itself begins, the Pardoner softens
up his audience with some ghastly moral anecdotes about various sins. He
concentrates especially on the three that his actual story will feature:
drunkenness and gluttony, gambling, and swearing and blasphemy. His
story is aimed at getting his audience to repent such evils ways; it is also
good for business. For, when he has finished, he tries to sell his 'holy' relics
and pardons, and is rudely put in his place by Harry Bailey.

Here, then, is the Pardoner's story of greed and murder. We suggest you
read the Summary first to be able to follow the sequence of events. Then,
either with the tape recording or, better, by reading Chaucer's words aloud
with your teacher, hear the whole story. The modern translation is there to
help you understand any difficult passages.

Summary of the Tale

lines 375–424	Three young men, already the worse for drink by noon, hear the bell ringing for a corpse being carried past the tavern. They enquire who is dead and learn it is their friend, killed by Death. They swear to look for Death and kill it.
lines 425–481	They meet a pitiful old man who is also looking for Death – not, like the three drunks, to destroy it, but in order to embrace it for he wants to die but feels condemned to a permanent and miserable old age. He directs the three men along a crooked path to find Death.
lines 482–519	In fact, they find a heap of gold coins and feel as lucky as lottery winners. Then, one of them proposes they draw lots for who should go and fetch food and drink while the others guard their treasure. The youngest draws the short straw and sets off for town.
lines 520–550	One of the remaining two suggests to the other that they should kill the youngest when he returns by stabbing him during a sham wrestling match. Then they can split the gold between themselves.
lines 551–592	Meanwhile, the youngest plans to kill the other two! He buys some poison from an apothecary (chemist), borrows some bottles, laces the drink with poison in two of them and fills the third with drink for himself. He then returns to his 'friends'.
lines 593–608	The two others kill him, refresh themselves from one of the poisoned bottles, and so die themselves.

'The Gambler' from Holbein's *Dance of Death*.

FROM: THE PARDONER'S TALE

Thise riotoures thre of whiche I telle,
Longe erst er prime rong of my belle,
Were set hem in a taverne for to drinke,
And as they sat, they herde a belle clinke
Biforn a cors, was caried to his grave.
380 That oon of hem gan callen to his knave:
'Go bet,' quod he, 'and axe redily
What cors is this that passeth heer forby;
And looke that thou reporte his name weel.'
'Sire,' quod this boy, 'it nedeth never-a-deel;
It was me toold er ye cam heer two houres.
He was, pardee, an old felawe of youres;
And sodeynly he was yslain to-night,
Fordronke, as he sat on his bench upright.
Ther cam a privee theef men clepeth Deeth,
390 That in this contree al the peple sleeth,
And with his spere he smoot his herte atwo,
And wente his wey withouten wordes mo.
He hath a thousand slain this pestilence.
And, maister, er ye come in his presence,
Me thinketh that it were necessarie
For to be war of swich an adversarie.
Beth redy for to meete him everemoore;
Thus taughte me my dame; I sey namoore.'
'By seinte Marie,' seyde this taverner,
400 'The child seith sooth, for he hath slain this
yeer,
Henne over a mile, withinne a greet village,
Bothe man and womman, child and hine, and
page;
I trowe his habitacioun be there.
To been avised greet wisdom it were,
Er that he dide a man dishonour.'
'Ye, Goddes armes!' quod this riotour,
'Is it swich peril with him for to meete?
I shal him seke by wey and eek by strete,
I make avow to Goddes digne bones!
410 Herkneth, felawes, we thre been al ones;
Lat ech of us holde up his hand til oother,
And ech of us bicomen otheres brother,
And we wol sleen this false traitour Deeth.
He shal be slain, he that so manye sleeth,
By Goddes dignitee, er it be night.'

The three loose-livers of whom I'm to tell,
A long while before the first matin bell
Had seated themselves in a tavern, drinking,
And, as they sat, they heard a handbell
clinking—
A corpse was being carried to its grave.
At this one of them called his serving-lad:
'Ask who it is,' said he, 'and look alive!
Run and find out whose corpse is passing by:
And see you get his name.' 'Sir,' said the boy,
'There is no need at all for me to go;
I was told before you came, two hours ago.
And he, indeed, was an old friend of yours.
He was killed last night, all of a sudden, as
He sat up on his bench, blind drunk. There
came
A softly treading thief, Death is his name,
Who's killing everybody everywhere,
And cut his heart in pieces with a spear,
And thereupon made off without a word.
Thousands he's killed, in the plague raging
here.
If I were you sir, I'd be on my guard
Before I went near such an adversary!
Always be ready to meet him anywhere—
My mother taught me that; I can't say more.'
The innkeeper broke in, 'By St Mary!
What the child says is true; he's killed this
year
In a big village over a mile from here
Every man, woman, child, workman and boy.
That's where he's living now, I'm pretty sure.
The wisest thing's to keep a good look-out,
Or else he's like to do a fellow dirt.'
'God's arms!' exclaimed one of these
debauchees,
'Is the fellow then so dangerous to meet?
In highways and in byways, street by street,
I'll seek him out, I vow it on God's bones.
Now listen, fellows: let us three be one,
Each of us hold his hand up to the other,
And each of us become the other's brother,
And we will kill this black betrayer, Death,
And kill the killer, By God's holy breath,
And that before the sun goes down on us!'

Togidres han thise thre hir trouthes plight
To live and dien ech of hem for oother,
As though he were his owene ybore brother.
And up they stirte, al dronken in this rage,
420 And forth they goon towardes that village
Of which the taverner hadde spoke biforn.
And many a grisly ooth thanne han they
    sworn,
And Cristes blessed body al torente—
Deeth shal be deed, if that they may him
    hente.
    Whan they han goon nat fully half a mile,
Right as they wolde han troden over a stile,
An oold man and a povre with hem mette,
This olde man ful mekely hem grette,
And seyde thus, 'Now, lordes, God yow see!'
430   The proudeste of thise riotoures three
Answerde again, 'What, carl, with sory grace!
Why artow al forwrapped save thy face?
Why livestow so longe in so greet age?'
    This olde man gan looke in his visage,
And seyde thus: 'For I ne kan nat finde
A man, though that I walked into Inde,
Neither in citee ne in no village,
That wolde chaunge his youthe for myn age;
And therfore moot I han myn age stille,
440 As longe time as it is Goddes wille.
Ne Deeth, allas, ne wol nat han my lyf.
Thus walke I, lyk a restelees kaitif,
And on the ground, which is my moodres
    gate,
I knokke with my staf, bothe erly and late,
And seye, "Leeve mooder, leet me in!
Lo how I vanisshe, flessh and blood and skin!
Allas! whan shul my bones been at reste?
Mooder, with yow wolde I chaunge my
    cheste
That in my chambre longe time hath be,
450 Ye, for an heyre clowt to wrappe in me."
But yet to me she wol nat do that grace,
For which ful pale and welked is my face.

They pledged their word, the three of them
    together,
That they would live and die for one another,
As though each were the other's own born
    brother.
And up they jumped in frenzied drunken rage,
Set off in the direction of that village
The innkeeper had spoken of before.
Many and gruesome were the oaths they
    swore,
Tearing Christ's body limb from limb,
Death shall be dead, if only they can catch
    him!
    When they'd not gone as much as half a
    mile,
Just as they were about to cross a stile
They met a poor old man, who greeted them
Humbly—'God save and keep you,
    gentlemen!'
    But the most insolent of these three rakes
Answered him back: 'Be damned to you, you
    wretch!
Why so wrapped up, and muffled to the eyes?
And why live on so long in such dotage?'
    The old man looked at him hard in the face,
And said, 'It is because I cannot find
Anyone, though I walked to the world's end,
In any city or in any village,
Who would exchange his youth for my old
    age.
And therefore I must stay an old man still
For just so long as it is in heaven's will.
Not even Death, alas, will take my life!
So, like a restless prisoner I pace,
And on the earth, which is my mother's gate,
Go knocking with my staff early and late,
Saying, "My dearest mother, let me in!
See how I wither, flesh, and blood, and skin!
Alas, when will my poor bones be at rest?
Dear mother, I would barter my strongbox
That's stood so long a time within my room,
Just for a haircloth shroud to wrap me in!"
But she will not do me that favour yet,
And so I bear a pale and withered face.

'But sires, to yow it is no curteisye
To speken to an old man vileynye,
But he trespasse in word, or elles in dede.
In Hooly Writ ye may yourself wel rede:
"Agains an oold man, hoor upon his heed,
Ye sholde arise;" wherfore I yeve yow reed,
Ne dooth unto an oold man noon harm now,
460 Namoore than that ye wolde men did to yow
In age, if that ye so longe abide.
And God be with yow, where ye go or ride!
I moot go thider as I have to go.'
   'Nay, olde cherl, by God, thou shalt nat so,'
Seyde this oother hasardour anon;
'Thou partest nat so lightly, by Seint John!
Thou spak right now of thilke traitour Deeth,
That in this contree alle oure freendes sleeth.
Have heer my trouthe, as thou art his espye,
470 Telle where he is, or thou shalt it abye,
By God, and by the hooly sacrement!
For soothly thou art oon of his assent
To sleen us yonge folk, thou false theef!'
   'Now, sires,' quod he, 'if that yow be so leef
To finde Deeth, turne up this croked wey,
For in that grove I lafte him, by my fey,
Under a tree, and there he wole abide;
Noght for youre boost he wole him no thing
   hide.
Se ye that ook? Right there ye shal him finde.
480 God save yow, that boghte again mankinde,
And yow amende.' Thus seyde this olde man;
And everich of thise riotoures ran
Til he cam to that tree, and ther they founde
Of florins fine of gold ycoined rounde
Wel ny an eighte busshels, as hem thoughte.
No lenger thanne after Deeth they soughte,
But ech of hem so glad was of that sighte,
For that the florins been so faire and brighte,
That doun they sette hem by this precious
   hoord.
490 The worste of hem, he spak the firste word.

'But sirs, it is not courteous of you
To speak so roughly to an old man, who
Has not offended you by word or deed.
It's there in Holy Writ for you to read:
"Thou shalt rise up before the hoary head
Of an old man"—and therefore do no harm,
I warn you, to an old man while you're
   young,
Any more than you'd like to have it done
To you in old age, should you live so long.
Now God be with you! I go where I must
   go.'
   'By God you shall not! Not so fast, old
   fellow,'
The second of the gamblers answered him:
'You shan't get off so easily, by St John!
You spoke just now about that ruffian Death
Who's killing all our friends the country
   round.
My word on it, as sure as you're his spy,
You'd best tell me where he is, or else you'll
   pay,
By God and His holy sacrament!
It's clear that you and he are in agreement
To kill young folk like us, you bloody cheat.'
   'Well, gentlemen,' said he, 'if you're so keen
To find out Death, turn up this winding road,
For on my word I left him in that grove
Under a tree, and there he will abide.
For all your braggadocio he'll not hide.
See that oak there? Right underneath you'll
   find
Death. God be with you, Who redeemed
   mankind,
And save you and amend!' said the old man.
And thereupon all three began to run
Until they reached the tree, and there they
   found
Gold florins, newly minted, fine and round,
And near eight bushels of them, so they
   thought.
Thenceforth it was no longer Death they
   sought,
Each of them was so happy at the sight,
Those florins looked so beautiful and bright.
They set themselves down by the precious
   hoard.
It was the worst of them spoke the first word.

'Bretheren,' quod he, 'taak kep what that I
seye;
My wit is greet, though that I bourde and
pleye.
This tresor hath Fortune unto us yiven,
In mirthe and joliftee oure lyf to liven,
And lightly as it comth, so wol we spende.
Ey! Goddes precious dignitee! who wende
To-day that we sholde han so fair a grace?
But mighte this gold be caried fro this place
Hoom to myn hous—or elles unto youres
500   (For wel ye woot that al this gold is oures)—
Thanne were we in heigh felicitee.
But trewely, by daye it may nat bee.
Men wolde seyn that we were theves stronge,
And for oure owene tresor doon us honge.
This tresor moste ycaried be by nighte
As wisely and as slyly as it mighte.
Wherfore I rede that cut among us alle
Be drawe, and lat se wher the cut wol falle;
And he that hath the cut with herte blithe
510   Shal renne to the town, and that ful swithe,
And bringe us breed and wyn ful prively.
And two of us shul kepen subtilly
This tresor wel; and if he wol nat tarie,
Whan it is night, we wol this tresor carie,
By oon assent, where as us thinketh best.'
Than oon of hem the cut broghte in his fest,
And bad hem drawe, and looke where it wol
falle;
And it fil on the yongeste of hem alle,
And forth toward the toun he wente anon.

'Brothers,' he said, 'mark what I've got to
say:
Although I play the fool, I'm pretty fly.
Upon us Fortune has bestowed this treasure
So we can live in luxury for ever.
We'll spend it   easy come, and easy go!
Whew! Holy God, but who would guess or
know
That we'd have such a slice of luck today?
If only we could get this gold away,
And carry it to my house, or to yours,
—I needn't say that all this gold is ours—
We'd be in clover, happy as can be!
But obviously it can't be done by day.
People would say that we were downright
thieves,
And for our rightful treasure, have us hung!
It is at night this treasure must be moved,
With every care and cunning, if we can.
And therefore this is my advice—let's all
Draw lots, and then see where the lot shall
fall;
And he who draws the shortest straw shall
run
Fast as he can, rejoicing, to the town,
And on the quiet buy us bread and wine.
The other two must keep a sharp look-out
And guard the gold; and if no time is lost,
We'll carry off the treasure when it's dark,
Take it wherever we decide is best.'
The speaker held the straws in his closed fist,
Told them to draw, and see where the luck
fell;
And it fell to the youngest of them all,
And he set off at once towards the town.

The Pardoner

520 And also soone as that he was gon,
That oon of hem spak thus unto that oother:
'Thow knowest wel thou art my sworen
　brother;
Thy profit wol I telle thee anon.
Thou woost wel that oure felawe is agon.
And heere is gold, and that ful greet plentee,
That shal departed been among us thre.
But nathelees, if I kan shape it so
That it departed were among us two,
Hadde I nat doon a freendes torn to thee?'
530　That oother answerde, 'I noot how that may
　be.
He woot wel that the gold is with us tweye;
What shal we doon? What shal we to him
　seye?'
　'Shal it be conseil?' seyde the firste shrewe,
'And I shal tellen in a wordes fewe.
What we shal doon, and bringe it wel
　aboute.'
　'I graunte,' quod that oother, 'out of doute,
That, by my trouthe, I wol thee nat biwreye.'
　'Now,' quod the firste, 'thou woost wel we
　be tweye,
And two of us shul strenger be than oon.
540 Looke whan that he is set, that right anoon
Aris as though thou woldest with him pleye,
And I shal rive him thurgh the sides tweye
Whil that thou strogelest with him as in game,
And with thy daggere looke thou do the same;
And thanne shal al this gold departed be,
My deere freend, bitwixen me and thee.
Thanne may we bothe our lustes all fulfille,
And pleye at dees right at oure owene wille.'
And thus acorded been thise shrewes tweye
550 To sleen the thridde, as ye han herd me seye.
　This yongeste, which that wente to the toun,
Ful ofte in herte he rolleth up and doun
The beautee of thise florins newe and
　brighte.
'O Lord!' quod he, 'if so were that I mighte
Have al this tresor to myself allone,
Ther is no man that liveth under the trone
Of God that sholde live so murye as I.'
And atte laste the feend, oure enemy,
Putte in his thought that he sholde poison beye,
560 With which he mighte sleen his felawes tweye;
For-why the feend foond him in swich livinge
That he hadde leve him to sorwe bringe.

And thereupon, so soon as he was gone,
One of the two who stayed said to the other:
'You know, of course, that you are my sworn
　brother.
I'll tell you something that you won't lose by.
As you can see, our friend has gone away,
And here is gold, and that in greatest plenty,
All waiting to be split between us three.
How would it be, if I can work it so
That it is only shared between us two,
Wouldn't I be doing you a friendly turn?'
　'But,' said the other, 'how can it be done?
He knows quite well the gold is with us here.
What shall we do? What shall we say to him?'
　Said the first villain: 'Now, can you keep
　mum?
I'll tell you in a word what's to be done,
All we need to do to bring it safely off.'
　'I'm on,' returned the other. 'My word on
　it,
Never you worry, I won't let you down.'
　'Now,' said the first, 'you know that we are
　two,
And two of us are stronger than just one.
Wait till he's settled, and when he sits down
Jump up, as if to grapple him in joke,
And I will skewer him right through the back
While you are scuffling with him as in fun—
And with your dagger see you do the same.
And when it's over, all this gold shall be
Shared out, dear fellow, between you and me.
Then each of us can follow his own bent,
Gaming and dicing to his heart's content.'
And thus it was this precious pair agreed,
As you've just heard me tell, to kill the third.
　The youngest—the one going to the town—
Keeps turning over and over in his mind
Those lovely shining florins, new and bright.
'O Lord!' exclaimed he, 'if I only might
Keep all that treasure for myself alone,
There's none alive beneath the heavenly
　throne
Of God, who'd live as happily as I!'
And then at last the Fiend, our enemy,
Put it into his head to go and buy
Poison with which to murder both his friends.
You see, such was the life he led, the Fiend
Had leave to bring him to an evil end.

For this was outrely his fulle entente,
To sleen hem bothe, and nevere to repente.
And forth he gooth, no lenger wolde he tarie,
Into the toun, unto a pothecarie,
And preyde him that he him wolde selle
Som poison, that he mighte his rattes quelle;
And eek ther was a polcat in his hawe,
570   That, as he seyde, his capouns hadde yslawe,
And fain he wolde wreke him, if he mighte,
On vermin that destroyed him by nighte.
    The pothecarie answerde, 'And thou shalt
     have
A thing that, also God my soule save,
In al this world ther is no creature,
That eten or dronken hath of this confiture
Noght but the montance of a corn of whete,
That he ne shal his lif anon forlete;
Ye, sterve he shal, and that in lasse while
580   Than thou wolt goon a paas nat but a mile,
This poisoun is so strong and violent.'
    This cursed man hath in his hond yhent
This poisoun in a box, and sith he ran
Into the nexte strete unto a man,
And borwed of him large botelles thre;
And in the two his poison poured he;
The thridde he kepte clene for his drinke.
For al the night he shoop him for to swinke
In caryinge of the gold out of that place.
590   And whan this riotour, with sory grace,
Hadde filled with wyn his grete botels thre,
To his felawes again repaireth he.
    What nedeth it to sermone of it moore?
For right as they hadde cast his deeth bifoore,
Right so they han him slain, and that anon.
And whan that this was doon, thus spak that
    oon:
'Now lat us sitte and drinke, and make us
    merie,
And afterward we wol his body berie.'
And with that word it happed him, par cas,
600   To take the botel ther the poison was,
And drank, and yaf his felawe drinke also,
For which anon they storven bothe two.
  But certes, I suppose that Avycen
Wroot nevere in no canon, ne in no fen,
Mo wonder signes of empoisoning
Than hadde thise wrecches two, er hir
    ending.
Thus ended been thise homicides two,
And eek the false empoisonere also.

Because it plainly was his fixed intent
To kill them both, and never to repent.
So off he goes with no more loss of time
To find an apothecary in the town.
He asked the man if he would sell him
    poison,
He wanted it for putting his rats down;
Also there was a polecat in his yard
That had killed all his chickens, so he said;
For if he could he'd like to get back at
The vermin that despoiled him day and night.
    The apothecary told him: 'You shall have
A thing so strong that, as my soul's to save,
In the whole world there is no living creature
Which, if it swallows any of this mixture,
No bigger amount than a grain of wheat,
But must then lose its life upon the spot;
Yes, it must die, and that in a less while,
Believe me, than it takes to walk a mile:
This poison is so strong and virulent.'
    The wretch reached out his hand for it and
    went,
Taking the poison with him in a box.
He hurried to a man in the next street,
From whom he borrowed three large bottles.
Then he poured the poison into two of them,
And for his own drink kept the third one
    clean,
Because he had made up his mind to work
Throughout the night at carrying off the gold.
And when—the devil fetch him!—he had filled
His three great bottles to the brim with wine,
He made his way back to his friends again.
    What need is there for sermonising further?
Just as they'd planned his murder earlier,
They killed him on the spot; when this was
    done,
The first said to the other, 'Let's sit down
And drink and celebrate; and after that
We'll bury him.' By chance, as he said this,
He took the bottle where the poison was,
And drank, and gave it to his friend to drink,
And thereupon they both died on the spot.
  Avicenna himself has not set down
In any section of his book, *The Canon
Of Medicine*—or so I would suppose—
Symptoms of poisoning more dire than those
The wretched pair endured in their last hours.
Such was the end of the two murderers,
And of the treacherous poisoner as well.

JOHN CLARE, *1793–1864*

John Clare became known as the Northamptonshire Peasant Poet when his first collection, 'Poems Descriptive of Rural Life and Scenery', was published in 1820. He was born the son of an agricultural labourer but his parents, particularly his mother, who was herself illiterate, were determined he should receive some education. He was taught his letters and numbers in dame school and later he had some tuition from two local schoolmasters.

It was at school that he met his first love, the fair haired, blue-eyed Mary Joyce of whom he wrote in his Autobiography:

'. . . my first attachment being a schoolboy affection was for Mary who . . . was beloved with a romantic or Platonic sort of feeling if I could but gaze upon her face or fancy a smile on her countenance I went away satisfyd we played with each other but named nothing of love yet I fancyd her eyes told me her affections . . . yet young as my heart was it would turn chill when I touchd her hand & tremble & I fancyd her feelings were the same for as I gazd earnestly in her face a tear would hang in her smiling eye & she would turn to wipe it away. Her heart was as tender as a bird's.'

His love of books was fostered by his teachers one of whom gave him the run of his library. He was too poor to buy books of his own and was 13 before he managed to acquire two: Dr Watts' 'Hymns and Spiritual Songs' and James Thomson's 'The Seasons'. He had been composing poems himself for two or three years already so it is no surprise that his first two purchases were books of verse.

In his 'Sketches' Clare describes the excitement of buying 'The Seasons'. Having read a little of the poem in a friend's copy he persuaded his father to give him one and sixpence (a quarter of a week's wages) to buy his own from the bookseller in Stamford. He couldn't wait to read his new volume and was entranced:

'On my return the sun got up . . . and as I did not like to let anyone see me reading on the road of a working day, I clumb over the wall into Burghley Park, and nestled in a lawn at the wall side.'

Reading and writing were regarded with suspicion by some of his neighbours who had little time for one who tried to better himself in this way: he was seen as 'getting above his station'. The publication of his first book of verse and his meeting with literary figures of the day at his publisher's in London, meant that he didn't fit in with the small world of the village: yet it was on the village and the surrounding countryside that his poetry depended. Few writers have as good an eye as Clare for the detail of the countryside, its changing seasons, its trees and flowers, its wildlife and the country-dwellers themselves. He was quite remarkably observant and he writes what he sees in a direct and honest way. The 'voice' of his poems is instantly recognisable.

Despite poverty, loneliness and many difficulties he continued to write. In 1820 he had married Patty Turner who did her level best to support him and a growing family. He wrote prolifically during this period, publishing 'The Shepherd's Calender' in 1824. All might have been well but in 1837 he was struck down by severe mental illness in which a form of epilepsy seems to have been associated with fits of manic depression. After a breakdown he entered an asylum in Epping Forest as a voluntary patient and, following a brief return to his home, he was finally committed to the Northampton Asylum in 1841 and remained there for the rest of his days. From earliest childhood he had loved Mary Joyce and her name frequently appears in poems of this later period. He continued to write both in Epping and Northampton and his poem which begins 'I am! yet what I am who cares or knows?' is both a testament to his genius and a profoundly moving poem.

WRITTEN IN NORTHAMPTON COUNTY ASYLUM

I AM! yet what I am who cares, or knows?
My friends forsake me like a memory lost.
I am the self-consumer of my woes;
   They rise and vanish, an oblivious host,
Shadows of life, whose very soul is lost.
And yet I am — I live — though I am toss'd

Into the nothingness of scorn and noise,
   Into the living sea of waking dream,
Where there is neither sense of life, nor joys,
   But the huge shipwreck of my own esteem
And all that's dear. Even those I loved the best
Are strange — nay, they are stranger than the rest.

I long for scenes where man has never trod —
   For scenes where women never smiled or wept —
There to abide with my Creator, God,
   And sleep as I in childhood sweetly slept,
Full of high thoughts, unborn. So let me lie, —
The grass below; above, the vaulted sky.

THE VIXEN

Among the taller wood with ivy hung,
The old fox plays and dances round her young.
She snuffs and barks if any passes by
And swings her tail and turns prepared to fly.
The horseman hurries by, she bolts to see,
And turns agen, from danger never free.
If any stands she runs among the poles
And barks and snaps and drives them in the holes.
The shepherd sees them and the boy goes by
And gets a stick and progs the hole to try.
They get all still and lie in safety sure,
And out again when everything's secure,
And start and snap at blackbirds bouncing by
To fight and catch the great white butterfly.

THE EVENING STAR

Hesperus!★ the day is gone,
Soft falls the silent dew,
A tear is now on many a flower
And heaven lives in you.

Hesperus! the evening mild
Falls round us soft and sweet.
'Tis like the breathings of a child
When day and evening meet.

Hesperus! the closing flower
Sleeps on the dewy ground,
While dew falls in a silent shower
And heaven breathes around.

Hesperus! thy twinkling ray
Beams in the blue of heaven,
And tells the traveller on his way
That Earth shall be forgiven!

★Another name for the evening star

PLEASANT SOUNDS

The rustling of leaves under the feet in woods and under
   hedges;
The crumping of cat-ice and snow down wood-rides, narrow
   lanes and every street causeway;
Rustling through a wood or rather rushing, while the wind
   halloos in the oak-top like thunder;
The rustle of birds' wings startled from their nests or flying
   unseen into the bushes;
The whizzing of larger birds overhead in a wood, such as
   crows, paddocks,★ buzzards;   ★ kites
The trample of robins and woodlarks on the brown leaves,
   and the patter of squirrels on the green moss;
The fall of an acorn on the ground, the pattering of nuts on
   the hazel branches as they fall from ripeness;
The flirt of ground-lark's wing from the stubbles — how
   sweet such pictures on dewy mornings, when the dew
   flashes from its brown feathers!

AN IDLE HOUR

Sauntering at ease I often love to lean
Oer old bridge walls and mark the flood below
Whose ripples through the weeds of oily green
Like happy travellers mutter as they go
And mark the sunshine dancing on the arch
Time keeping to the merry waves beneath
And on the banks see drooping blossoms parch
Thirsting for water in the days hot breath
Right glad of mud drops plashed upon their leaves
By cattle plunging from the steepy brink
While water flowers more than their share receive
And revel to their very cups in drink
Just like the world some strive and fare but ill
While others riot and have plenty still.

AUTUMN

I love the fitful gust that shakes
The casement all the day,
And from the glossy elm-tree takes
The faded leaves away,
Twirling them by the window pane
With thousand others down the lane.

I love to see the shaking twig
Dance till the shut of eve,
The sparrow on the cottage rig,
Whose chirp would make believe
That Spring was just now flirting by
In Summer's lap with flowers to lie.

I loved to see the cottage smoke
Curl upwards through the trees,
The pigeons nestled round the cote
On November days like these:
The cock upon the dunghill crowing,
The mill-sails on the heath a-going.

The feather from the raven's breast
Falls on the stubble lea,
The acorns near the old crow's nest
Drop pattering down the tree:
The grunting pigs that wait for all,
Scramble and hurry where they fall.

LOVE

Love lives beyond
The tomb, the earth, which fades like dew —
I love the fond,
The faithful, and the true.

Love lies in sleep,
The happiness of healthy dreams,
Eve's dews may weep,
But love delightful seems.

'Tis seen in flowers,
And in the even's pearly dew,
On earth's green hours,
And in the heaven's eternal blue.

'Tis heard in spring
When light and sunbeams, warm and kind,
On angel's wing
Brings love and music to the wind.

And where is voice
So young and beautifully sweet
As nature's choice,
When spring and lovers meet?

Love lives beyond
The tomb, the earth, the flowers, and dew.
I love the fond,
The faithful, young, and true.

TO MARY: IT IS THE EVENING HOUR

It is the evening hour,
   How silent all doth lie,
The hornèd moon he shews his face
   In the river with the sky.
Just by the path on which we pass
The flaggy lake lies still as glass.

Spirit of her I love,
   Whispering to me,
Stories of sweet visions, as I rove,
   Here stop, and crop with me
Sweet flowers that in the still hour grew,
We'll take them home, nor shake off the bright dew.

Mary, or sweet spirit of thee,
   As the bright sun shines to-morrow,
Thy dark eyes these flowers shall see,
   Gathered by me in sorrow,
In the still hour when my mind was free
To walk alone — yet wish I walk'd with thee.

ALFRED, LORD TENNYSON *1809–1892*

Alfred Tennyson was the fourth son in a typically large, Victorian middle-class family of twelve children – but his upbringing was not all ease and comfort. His father was disinherited in favour of a younger brother and had to make his living as a clergyman, a profession that he disliked. The Reverend George Tennyson's dissatisfaction with life no doubt contributed to his liking for alcohol but, though young Alfred would have witnessed violent bouts of drunkenness in his father, he also benefited from his father's considerable learning and tuition that prepared him for his studies at Cambridge. He had already started to write in his teens and, with his brother Charles, had even published a slim volume of poems. At Cambridge he continued to write, encouraged by a group called 'The Apostles'. The leader, Arthur Hallam, became a close friend but, sadly, was to die young – an event that Tennyson felt deeply and which influenced many of his poems, especially 'In Memoriam' published in 1850. In the same year, Tennyson became poet laureate in succession to Wordsworth and in 1884 he became a peer. During the last 40 years of his life he was the most popular and famous poet of the period, seeming to represent the Victorian age in his appearance as well as his poetry. He was a large man with a powerful physique, usually made more impressive by a cloak and broad-brimmed hat, and a booming voice when he read his poems that captivated his audiences.

The selection here includes poems about birds and monsters which show different moods – from the threatening horror of 'The Kraken', to the impressive superiority of 'The Eagle' and the light-hearted picture of 'Song – The Owl'. These poems, together with 'The Splendour Falls'; and 'Sweet and Low' also show Tennyson's skill in making the sounds of his words and the rhythms of the lines fit the subjects he is writing about. There is also a ballad and one of the best-known narrative poems in the language, 'The Lady of Shalott'. Tennyson's poems are known for their musical qualities, strong visual images and interesting stories – but he was also a thoughtful writer. The tiny poem 'Flower in the Crannied Wall', and his own 'poetic goodbye' to the world in 'Crossing the Bar' find him questioning the meaning of life and death.

THE EAGLE

He clasps the crag with hookéd hands;
Close to the sun in lonely lands,
Ringed with the azure world, he stands.

The wrinkled sea beneath him crawls;
He watches from his mountain walls,
And like a thunderbolt he falls.

THE KRAKEN*   ★a mythical sea beast of gigantic size.

Below the thunders of the upper deep,
Far, far beneath in the abysmal sea,
His ancient, dreamless, uninvaded sleep
The Kraken sleepeth: faintest sunlights flee
About his shadowy sides; above him swell
Huge sponges of millennial growth and height;
And far away into the sickly light,
From many a wondrous grot and secret cell
Unnumbered and enormous polypi★   ★ octopuses
Winnow with giant arms the slumbering green.
There hath he lain for ages, and will lie
Battening upon huge sea worms in his sleep,
Until the latter fire★ shall heat the deep;   ★fire that will finally consume the world.
Then once by man and angels to be seen,
In roaring he shall rise and on the surface die.

FLOWER IN THE CRANNIED WALL

Flower in the crannied wall,
I pluck you out of the crannies,
I hold you here, root and all, in my hand,
Little flower — but if I could understand
What you are, root and all, and all in all,
I should know what God and man is.

THE SPLENDOUR FALLS

The splendour falls on castle walls
    And snowy summits old in story:
The long light shakes across the lakes,
    And the wild cataract leaps in glory.
Blow, bugle, blow, set the wild echoes flying,
Blow, bugle; answer, echoes, dying, dying, dying.

O hark, O hear! how thin and clear,
    And thinner, clearer, farther going!
O sweet and far from cliff and scar
    The horns of Elfland faintly blowing!
Blow, let us hear the purple glens replying:
Blow, bugle; answer, echoes, dying, dying, dying.

O love, they die in yon rich sky,
    They faint on hill or field or river:
Our echoes roll from soul to soul,
    And grow for ever and for ever.
Blow, bugle, blow, set the wild echoes flying,
And answer, echoes, answer, dying, dying, dying.

FROM: THE PRINCESS

Sweet and low, sweet and low,
    Wind of the western sea,
Low, low, breathe and blow,
    Wind of the western sea!
Over the rolling waters go,
Come from the dying moon, and blow,
    Blow him again to me;
While my little one, while my pretty one, sleeps.

Sleep and rest, sleep and rest,
    Father will come to thee soon;
Rest, rest, on mother's breast,
    Father will come to thee soon;
Father will come to his babe in the nest,
Silver sails all out of the west
    Under the silver moon:
Sleep, my little one, sleep, my pretty one, sleep.

SONG—THE OWL

I

WHEN cats run home and light is come,
    And dew is cold upon the ground,
And the far-off stream is dumb,
    And the whirring sail goes round,
    And the whirring sail goes round;
        Alone and warming his five wits,
        The white owl in the belfry sits.

II

When merry milkmaids click the latch,
    And rarely smells the new-mown hay,
And the cock hath sung beneath the thatch
    Twice or thrice his roundelay,
    Twice or thrice his roundelay;
        Alone and warming his five wits,
        The white owl in the belfry sits.

LADY CLARE

It was the time when lilies blow,
    And clouds are highest up in air,
Lord Ronald brought a lily-white doe
    To give his cousin, Lady Clare.

I trow they did not part in scorn:
    Lovers long-betroth'd were they:
They two will wed the morrow morn:
    God's blessing on the day!

'He does not love me for my birth,
    Nor for my lands so broad and fair;
He loves me for my own true worth,
    And that is well,' said Lady Clare.

In there came old Alice the nurse,
    Said, 'Who was this that went from thee?'
'It was my cousin,' said Lady Clare.
    'To-morrow he weds with me.'

'O God be thank'd!' said Alice the nurse,
    'That all comes round so just and fair:
Lord Ronald is heir of all your lands,
    And you are not the Lady Clare'.

'Are ye out of your mind, my nurse, my nurse?'
    Said Lady Clare, 'that ye speak so wild?'
'As God's above,' said Alice the nurse,
    'I speak the truth: you are my child.

'The old Earl's daughter died at my breast;
    I speak the truth, as I live by bread!
I buried her like my own sweet child,
    And put my child in her stead.'

'Falsely, falsely, have ye done,
    O mother,' she said, 'if this be true,
To keep the best man under the sun
    So many years from his due.'

'Nay now, my child,' said Alice the nurse,
   'But keep the secret for your life,
And all you have will be Lord Ronald's,
   When you are man and wife.'

'If I'm a beggar born,' she said,
   'I will speak out, for I dare not lie.
Pull off, pull off, the brooch of gold,
   And fling the diamond necklace by.'

'Nay now, my child,' said Alice the nurse,
   'But keep the secret all ye can.'
She said 'Not so: but I will know
   If there be any faith in man.'

'Nay now, what faith?' said Alice the nurse,
   'The man will cleave unto his right.'
'And he shall have it,' the lady replied,
   'Tho' I should die to-night.'

'Yet give one kiss to your mother dear!
   Alas, my child, I sinn'd for thee.'
'O mother, mother, mother,' she said,
   'So strange it seems to me.

'Yet here's a kiss for my mother dear,
   My mother dear, if this be so,
And lay your hand upon my head,
   And bless me, mother, ere I go.'

She clad herself in a russet gown,
   She was no longer Lady Clare:
She went by dale, and she went by down,
   With a single rose in her hair.

The lily-white doe Lord Ronald had brought
   Leapt up from where she lay,
Dropt her head in the maiden's hand,
   And follow'd her all the way.

Down stept Lord Ronald from his tower:
   'O Lady Clare, you shame your worth!
Why come you drest like a village maid,
   That are the flower of the earth?'

'If I come drest like a village maid,
   I am but as my fortunes are:
I am a beggar born,' she said,
   'And not the Lady Clare.'

'Play me no tricks,' said Lord Ronald,
   'For I am yours in word and in deed.
Play me no tricks,' said Lord Ronald,
   'Your riddle is hard to read.'

O and proudly stood she up!
   Her heart within her did not fail:
She look'd into Lord Ronald's eyes,
   And told him all her nurse's tale.

He laugh'd a laugh of merry scorn:
   He turn'd and kiss'd her where she stood;
If you are not the heiress born,
   And I,' said he, 'the next in blood —

'If you are not the heiress born,
   And I', said he, 'the lawful heir,
We two will wed to-morrow morn,
   And you shall still be Lady Clare.'

THE LADY OF SHALOTT

PART I

On either side the river lie
Long fields of barley and of rye,
That clothe the wold and meet the sky;
And thro' the field the road runs by
    To many-tower'd Camelot;
And up and down the people go,
Gazing where the lilies blow
Round an island there below,
    The island of Shalott.

Willows whiten, aspens quiver,
Little breezes dusk and shiver
Thro' the wave that runs for ever
By the island in the river
    Flowing down to Camelot.
Four gray walls, and four gray towers,
Overlook a space of flowers,
And the silent isle imbowers
    The Lady of Shalott.

By the margin, willow-veil'd,
Slide the heavy barges trail'd
By slow horses; and unhail'd
The shallop flitteth silken-sail'd
    Skimming down to Camelot:
But who hath seen her wave her hand?
Or at the casement seen her stand?
Or is she known in all the land,
    The Lady of Shalott?

Only reapers, reaping early
In among the bearded barley,
Hear a song that echoes cheerly
From the river winding clearly,
    Down to tower'd Camelot:
And by the moon the reaper weary,
Lifting sheaves in uplands airy,
Listening, whispers ''Tis the fairy
    Lady of Shalott.'

PART II

There she weaves by night and day
A magic web with colours gay.
She has heard a whisper say,
A curse is on her if she stay
    To look down to Camelot.
She knows not what the curse may be,
And so she weaveth steadily,
And little other care hath she,
    The Lady of Shalott.

And moving thro' a mirror clear
That hangs before her all the year,
Shadows of the world appear.
There she sees the highway near
    Winding down to Camelot:
There the river eddy whirls,
And there the surly village-churls,
And the red cloaks of market girls,
    Pass onward from Shalott.

Sometimes a troop of damsels glad,
An abbot on an ambling pad,
Sometimes a curly shepherd-lad,
Or long-hair'd page in crimson clad,
    Goes by to tower'd Camelot;
And sometimes thro' the mirror blue
The knights come riding two and two:
She hath no loyal knight and true,
    The Lady of Shalott.

But in her web she still delights
To weave the mirror's magic sights,
For often thro' the silent nights
A funeral, with plumes and lights
    And music, went to Camelot:
Or when the moon was overhead,
Came two young lovers lately wed;
'I am half sick of shadows,' said
    The Lady of Shalott.

PART III
A bow-shot from her bower-eaves,
He rode between the barley-sheaves,
The sun came dazzling thro' the leaves,
And flamed upon the brazen greaves
    Of bold Sir Lancelot.
A red-cross knight for ever kneel'd
To a lady in his shield,
That sparkled on the yellow field,
    Beside remote Shalott.

The gemmy bridle glitter'd free,
Like to some branch of stars we see
Hung in the golden Galaxy.
The bridle bells rang merrily
    As he rode down to Camelot:
And from his blazon'd baldric slung
A mighty silver bugle hung,
And as he rode his armour rung,
    Beside remote Shalott.

All in the blue unclouded weather
Thick-jewell'd shone the saddle-leather,
The helmet and the helmet-feather
Burn'd like one burning flame together,
    As he rode down to Camelot.
As often thro' the purple night,
Below the starry clusters bright,
Some bearded meteor, trailing light,
    Moves over still Shalott.

His broad clear brow in sunlight glow'd;
On burnish'd hooves his war-horse trode;
From underneath his helmet flow'd
His coal-black curls as on he rode,
    As he rode down to Camelot.
From the bank and from the river
He flash'd into the crystal mirror,
'Tirra lirra,' by the river
    Sang Sir Lancelot.

She left the web, she left the loom,
She made three paces thro' the room,
She saw the water-lily bloom,
She saw the helmet and the plume,
    She look'd down to Camelot.
Out flew the web and floated wide;
The mirror crack'd from side to side;
'The curse is come upon me,' cried
    The Lady of Shalott.

PART IV
In the stormy east-wind straining,
The pale yellow woods were waning,
The broad stream in his banks complaining,
Heavily the low sky raining
    Over tower'd Camelot;
Down she came and found a boat
Beneath a willow left afloat,
And round about the prow she wrote
    The Lady of Shalott.

And down the river's dim expanse
Like some bold seer in a trance,
Seeing all his own mischance –
With a glassy countenance
    Did she look to Camelot.
And at the closing of the day
She loosed the chain, and down she lay;
The broad stream bore her far away,
    The Lady of Shalott.

Lying, robed in snowy white
That loosely flew to left and right –
The leaves upon her falling light –
Thro' the noises of the night
    She floated down to Camelot:
And as the boat-head wound along
The willowy hills and fields among,
They heard her singing her last song,
    The Lady of Shalott.

Heard a carol, mournful, holy,
Chanted loudly, chanted lowly,
Till her blood was frozen slowly,
And her eyes were darken'd wholly,
    Turn'd to tower'd Camelot.
For ere she reach'd upon the tide
The first house by the water-side,
Singing in her song she died,
    The Lady of Shalott.

Under tower and balcony,
By garden-wall and gallery,
A gleaming shape she floated by,
Dead-pale between the houses high,
    Silent into Camelot.
Out upon the wharfs they came,
Knight and burgher, lord and dame,
And round the prow they read her name
    The Lady of Shalott.

Who is this? and what is here?
And in the lighted palace near
Died the sound of royal cheer:
And they cross'd themselves for fear,
    All the knights at Camelot;
But Lancelot mused a little space;
He said, 'She has a lovely face;
God in his mercy lend her grace,
    The Lady of Shalott.'

CROSSING THE BAR*

*this poem was chosen by Tennyson
to be the last in his collection

Sunset and evening star,
    And one clear call for me!
And may there be no moaning of the bar,*
    When I put out to sea.

*mournful sound of the
sea on a sand bar at the
harbour mouth

But such a tide as moving seems asleep,
    Too full for sound and foam,
When that which drew from out the boundless deep
    Turns again home.

Twilight and evening bell,
    And after that the dark!
And may there be no sadness of farewell,
    When I embark;

For though from out our bourne* of Time and Place
    The flood may bear me far,
I hope to see my Pilot face to face
    When I have crossed the bar.

*boundary

EMILY DICKINSON *1830–1886*

'One of the oddest and most intriguing personalities in literary history' – so says Ted Hughes in his Introduction to a selection of Emily Dickinson's poems. Certainly, her life and her poetry are unusual. She lived virtually all her life in her family's homes in Amherst, Massachusetts. Apparently, she was a lively, humorous child but showed little interest in exploring beyond her immediate surroundings. She never married and, as she grew older, she confined herself increasingly to the household and her garden. Yet, if her physical world shrank, her imaginative world expanded. The extent of her writing was only realised long after her death: she wrote 1775 poems, many of them vivid miniatures as here, and saw only six of them published in her own lifetime.

Emily Dickinson remains a puzzle. She lived a very private, domestic life yet, far from being timid and fearful with people, she was a sociable, if rather intense, companion. Her poems show delight and excitement at all living things, yet they also contain frequent images of death. She writes about local and particular details, especially of the natural world, yet her poems often include strong, memorable images on a grand scale of the Earth and the Heavens. Her life and her poetry seem full of opposites, if not contradictions.

Ballads, hymns, riddles are the deceptively simple forms that influenced her work but, more than that of most poets, her style is her own invention. Her eccentric punctuation via dashes will not translate into the familiar commas and full stops. It is part of her language which, with the typically short lines, isolates key words. One writer has suggested that the words in Emily Dickinson's poems are like collections of brightly-coloured stones. As you read the poems, you will notice how many of them have a very sharp and narrow focus on the objects they describe; living things are observed with the scrutiny and intensity of a microscope.

The selection here begins with two poems about the wind. Listen to the poems read aloud and you will hear the wind's sounds, see its movements, sense its changing shapes and feel its force. There are some mysterious phrases and some vivid images such as Elijah riding away 'Upon a Wheel of Cloud' which stick in the mind. The wind is seen as a ghost, an Old Testament prophet, a monster. The three poems which follow focus on small, often secretive, creatures – a snake, a bird and a spider – all observed in careful detail and with a sense of the magic of creation. Next, there are two strange stories – an imaginary burglary and a dream-like fantasy about a walk by the sea. The last two poems are more difficult to understand because they deal with the journey from life to death, the end of which no-one knows – as the last line of the poem reminds us.

'LIKE RAIN IT SOUNDED TILL IT CURVED'

Like Rain it sounded till it curved
And then I knew 'twas Wind —
It walked as wet as any Wave
But swept as dry as sand —
When it had pushed itself away
To some remotest Plain
A coming as of Hosts was heard
That was indeed the Rain —
It filled the Wells, it pleased the Pools
It warbled in the Road —
It pulled the spigot from the Hills
And let the Floods abroad —
It loosened acres, lifted seas
The sites of Centres stirred
Then like Elijah rode away
Upon a Wheel of Cloud.

'AN AWFUL TEMPEST MASHED THE AIR'

An awful Tempest mashed the air —
The clouds were gaunt, and few —
A Black — as of a Spectre's Cloak
Hid Heaven and Earth from view.

The creatures chuckled on the Roofs —
And whistled in the air —
And shook their fists —
And gnashed their teeth—
And swung their frenzied hair.

The morning lit — the Birds arose —
The Monster's faded eyes
Turned slowly to his native coast —
And peace — was Paradise!

'A NARROW FELLOW IN THE GRASS'

A narrow Fellow in the Grass
Occasionally rides —
You may have met Him — did you not
His notice sudden is —

The Grass divides as with a Comb —
A spotted shaft is seen —
And then it closes at your feet
And opens further on —

He likes a Boggy Acre
A Floor too cool for Corn —
Yet when a Boy, and Barefoot —
I more than once at Noon
Have passed, I thought, a Whip lash
Unbraiding in the Sun
When stooping to secure it
It wrinkled, and was gone —

Several of Nature's People
I know, and they know me—
I feel for them a transport
Of cordiality —

But never met this Fellow
Attended, or alone
Without a tighter breathing
And Zero at the Bone —

'A BIRD CAME DOWN THE WALK'

A bird came down the walk:
He did not know I saw;
He bit an angle-worm in halves
And ate the fellow, raw.

And then he drank a dew
From a convenient grass,
And then hopped sidewise to the wall
To let a beetle pass.

He glanced with rapid eyes
That hurried all abroad, —
They looked like frightened beads,
    I thought
He stirred his velvet head

Like one in danger; cautious,
I offered him a crumb,
And he unrolled his feathers
And rowed him softer home

Than oars divide the ocean,
Too silver for a seam,
Or butterflies, off banks of noon,
Leap, plashless, as they swim.

'THE SPIDER HOLDS A SILVER BALL'

The Spider holds a Silver Ball
In unperceived Hands —
And dancing softly to Himself
His Yarn of Pearl — unwinds —

He plies from Nought to Nought —
In unsubstantial trade —
Supplants our Tapestries with His —
In half the period —

An Hour to rear supreme
His Continents of Light —
Then dangle from the Housewife's Broom —
His Boundaries — forgot —

'I KNOW SOME LONELY HOUSES OFF THE ROAD'

I know some lonely houses off the road
A robber'd like the look of, —
Wooden barred,
And windows hanging low,
Inviting to
A portico,

Where two could creep:
One hand the tools,
The other peep
To make sure all's asleep.
Old-fashioned eyes,
Not easy to surprise!

How orderly the kitchen'd look by night,
With just a clock, —
But they could gag the tick,
And mice won't bark;
And so the walls don't tell,
None will.

A pair of spectacles ajar just stir —
An almanac's aware.
Was it the mat winked,
Or a nervous star?
The moon slides down the stair
To see who's there.

There's plunder, — where?
Tankard, or spoon,
Earring, or stone,
A watch, some ancient brooch
To match the grandmamma,
Staid sleeping there.

Day rattles, too,
Stealth's slow;
The sun has got as far
As the third sycamore.
Screams chanticleer,
'Who's there?'

And echoes, trains away,
Sneer — 'Where?'
While the old couple, just astir,
Think that the sunrise left the door ajar!

'I STARTED EARLY, TOOK MY DOG'

I started early, took my dog,
    And visited the sea.
The mermaids in the basement
Came out to look at me

And frigates in the upper floor
    Extended hempen hands,
Presuming me to be a mouse
    Aground upon the sands,

But no man moved me till the tide
    Went past my simple shoe
And past my apron and my belt
    And past my bodice too,

And made as he would eat me up
    As wholly as a dew
Upon a dandelion's sleeve;
    And then I started too

And he, he followed close behind;
    I felt his silver heel
Upon my ankle, then my shoes
    Would overflow with pearl,

Until we met the solid town.
    No one he seemed to know
And bowing with a mighty look
    At me, the sea withdrew.

'BECAUSE I COULD NOT STOP FOR DEATH'

Because I could not stop for Death —
He kindly stopped for me —
The Carriage held but just Ourselves —
And Immortality.

We slowly drove — He knew no haste
And I had put away
My labor and my leisure too,
For His Civility —

We passed the School, where Children strove
At Recess — in the Ring —
We passed the Fields of Gazing Grain —
We passed the Setting Sun —

Or rather — He passed Us —
The Dews drew quivering and chill —
For only Gossamer, my Gown —
My Tippet — only Tulle —

We paused before a House that seemed
A Swelling of the Ground —
A Roof was scarcely visible —
The Cornice — in the Ground —

Since then — 'tis Centuries — and yet
Feels shorter than the Day
I first surmised the Horses' Heads
Were toward Eternity —

'I FELT A FUNERAL, IN MY BRAIN'

I felt a Funeral, in my Brain,
And Mourners to and fro
Kept treading — treading — till it seemed
That Sense was breaking through —

And when they all were seated,
A Service, like a Drum —
Kept beating — beating — till I thought
My Mind was going numb —

And then I heard them lift a Box
And creak across my Soul
With those same Boots of Lead, again,
Then space — began to toll,

As all the Heavens were a Bell,
And Being, but an Ear,
And I, and Silence, some strange Race
Wrecked, solitary here —

And then a Plank in Reason, broke,
And I dropped down, and down —
And hit a World, at every plunge,
And Finished knowing — then —

D H LAWRENCE 1885–1930

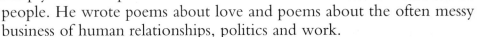

DH Lawrence is better known as a writer of novels, but he was also a considerable poet. He started writing poems when he was 16 and his first poems were published in 1910 when he was a young schoolmaster of 24. Over the remaining 20 years of his life he wrote and published many more poems.

His early poems were in rhymed verse and some in the dialect of his native Nottinghamshire. Soon he abandoned the strict conventions of traditional verse for free verse poems which might spread over many lines. He wrote carefully observed poems about animals and the natural world and he wrote equally sharply observed pieces about the behaviour of people. He wrote poems about love and poems about the often messy business of human relationships, politics and work.

As a child living in a pit village surrounded by open country he had a close knowledge of both the industrial and the rural ways of life: two contrasting worlds. His father was a nearly illiterate coal miner and his mother a determined woman of some education who had higher aspirations for her sons than that they should follow their father down the pit: two more contrasting worlds. Lawrence trained as a teacher and earned two pounds a week in his first post, but his great success as a writer soon took him into the most privileged circles of society. Again he had access to another quite different world. With such a wide and varied experience, it is not surprising that many of his poems are concerned with issues of class and wealth.

Whatever he wrote about it was with passion, directness and total honesty. There is a vividness and passion about his writing which reflected the intense way he lived his own life. He felt strongly that most people were trapped by the modern world into the boring, repetitive and numbing daily round of being wage-slaves and many of his later poems condemn this aspect of industrial society. Even the wealthy who were not trapped in this way, seemed to him to be trapped by material things, by possessions. Either way, the life had gone out of things, the spirit had been dulled.

We can give only a few examples of his verse here. The tender dialect poem 'Violets' (p. 187) was written early in his career. So too was 'Last Lesson of the Afternoon' (p. 183) in which Lawrence recalls the weariness of trying to interest his class in their work. The remarkable free verse poem 'Bat' (p. 184) is one of many which show his gift for detailed observation and feeling for the natural world. Finally a group of poems about human beings and their work shows his strong feelings about the modern world.

LAST LESSON OF THE AFTERNOON

When will the bell ring, and end this weariness?
How long have they tugged the leash, and strained apart,
My pack of unruly hounds! I cannot start
Them again on a quarry of knowledge they hate to hunt,
I can haul them and urge them no more.

No longer now can I endure the brunt
Of the books that lie out on the desks; a full threescore
Of several insults of blotted pages, and scrawl
Of slovenly work that they have offered me.
I am sick, and what on earth is the good of it all?
What good to them or me, I cannot see!

      So, shall I take
My last dear fuel of life to heap on my soul
And kindle my will to a flame that shall consume
Their dross of indifference; and take the toll
Of their insults in punishment? — I will not! —

I will not waste my soul and my strength for this.
What do I care for all that they do amiss!
What is the point of this teaching of mine, and of this
Learning of theirs? It all goes down the same abyss.

What does it matter to me, if they can write
A description of a dog, or if they can't?
What is the point? To us both, it is all my aunt!
And yet I'm supposed to care, with all my might.

I do not, and will not; they won't and they don't;
 and that's all!
I shall keep my strength for myself; they can keep
 theirs as well.
Why should we beat our heads against the wall
Of each other? I shall sit and wait for the bell.

BABY RUNNING BAREFOOT

When the white feet of the baby beat across the grass
The little white feet nod like white flowers in a wind,
They poise and run like puffs of wind that pass
Over water where the weeds are thinned.

And the sight of their white playing in the grass
Is winsome as a robin's song, so fluttering:
Or like two butterflies that settle on a glass
Cup for a moment, soft little wing-beats uttering.

And I wish that the baby would tack across here to me
Like a wind-shadow running on a pond, so she could stand
With two little bare white feet upon my knee
And I could feel her feet in either hand

Cool as syringa buds in morning hours,
Or firm and silken as young peony flowers.

BAT

At evening, sitting on this terrace,
When the sun from the west, beyond Pisa, beyond the
    mountains of Carrara
Departs, and the world is taken by surprise. . .

When the tired flower of Florence is in gloom beneath the
    glowing
Brown hills surrounding. . .
When under the arches of the Ponte Vecchio
A green light enters against stream, flush from the west,
Against the current of obscure Arno. . .

Look up, and you see things flying
Between the day and the night;
Swallows with spools of dark thread sewing the shadows
    together.

A circle swoop, and a quick parabola under the bridge arches
Where light pushes through;
A sudden turning upon itself of a thing in the air.
A dip to the water.

And you think:
'The swallows are flying so late!'

Swallows?

Dark air-life looping
Yet missing the pure loop. . .
A twitch, a twitter, an elastic shudder in flight
And serrated wings against the sky,
Like a glove, a black glove thrown up at the light,
And falling back.

Never swallows!
Bats!
The swallows are gone.

At a wavering instant the swallows give way to bats
By the Ponte Vecchio. . .
Changing guard.

Bats, and an uneasy creeping in one's scalp
As the bats swoop overhead!
Flying madly.

Pipistrello!
Black piper on a infinitesimal pipe.
Little lumps that fly in air and have voices indefinite, wildly
    vindictive;

Wings like bits of umbrella.

Bats!

Creatures that hang themselves up like an old rag, to sleep;
And disgustingly upside down.
Hanging upside down like rows of disgusting old rags
And grinning in their sleep.
Bats!

In China the bat is symbol of happiness.

Not for me!

WAGES

The wages of work is cash.
The wages of cash is want more cash.
The wages of want more cash is vicious competition.
The wages of vicious competition is   the world we live in.

The work–cash–want circle is the viciousest circle
that ever turned men into fiends.

Earning a wage is a prison occupation
and a wage-earner is a sort of gaol-bird.
Earning a salary is a prison overseer's job,
a gaoler instead of a gaol-bird.

Living on your income is strolling grandly outside the
     prison
in terror lest you have to go in. And since the work-prison
     covers
almost every scrap of the living earth, you stroll up and
     down
on a narrow beat, about the same as a prisoner taking his
     exercise.

This is called universal freedom.

NEW HOUSES, NEW CLOTHES

New houses, new furniture, new streets, new clothes, new
     sheets
everything new and machine-made sucks life out of us
and makes us cold, makes us lifeless
the more we have.

THINGS MEN HAVE MADE

Things men have made with wakened hands, and put soft
     life into
are awake through years with transferred touch, and go
     on glowing
for long years.
And for this reason, some old things are lovely
warm still with the life of forgotten men who made them.

VIOLETS

Sister, tha knows while we was on th' planks
   Aside o' t' grave, an' th' coffin set
On th' yaller clay, wi' th' white flowers top of it
   Waitin' ter be buried out o' th' wet?

An' t' parson makin' haste, an' a' t' black
   Huddlin' up i' t' rain,
Did t' 'appen ter notice a bit of a lass way back
   Hoverin', lookin' poor an' plain?

   — How should I be lookin' round!
     An' me standin' there on th' plank,
   An' our Ted's coffin set on th' ground,
     Waitin' to be sank!

   I'd as much as I could do, to think
     Of 'im bein' gone
   That young, an' a' the fault of drink
     An' carryin's on! —

Let that be; 'appen it worna th' drink, neither,
Nor th' carryin' on as killed 'im.
               —No, 'appen not,
My sirs! But I say 'twas! For a blither
Lad never stepped, till 'e got in with your lot. —

All right, all right, it's my fault! But let
Me tell about that lass. When you'd all gone
Ah stopped behind on t' pad, i' t' pourin' wet
An' watched what 'er 'ad on.

Tha should ha' seed 'er slive up when yer'd gone!
Tha should ha' seed 'er kneel an' look in
At th' sloppy grave! an' 'er little neck shone
That white, an' 'er cried that much, I'd like to begin

Scraightin' mysen as well. 'Er undid 'er black
Jacket at th' bosom, an' took out
Over a double 'andful o' violets, a' in a pack
An' white an' blue in a ravel, like a clout.

An' warm, for th' smell come waftin' to me. 'Er put 'er face
Right in 'em, an' scraighted a bit again,
Then after a bit 'er dropped 'em down that place,
An' I come away, acause o' th' teemin' rain.

But I thowt ter mysen, as that wor th' only bit
O' warmth as 'e got down theer; th' rest wor stone cold.
From that bit of a wench's bosom; 'e'd be glad of it,
Gladder nor of thy lilies, if tha maun be told.

PHOEBE HESKETH, 1909–

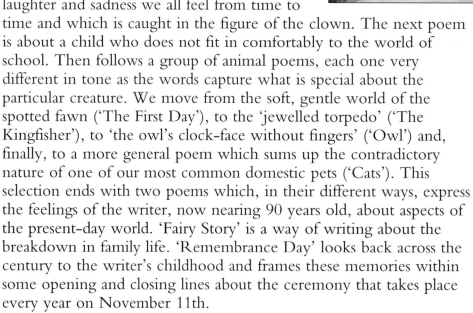

Phoebe Hesketh began writing poems before the Second World War and now, more than 50 years later, she is still writing with energy and enthusiasm. She was born in Preston, Lancashire and educated at Cheltenham Ladies' College. She married in 1931, had three children and has lived most of her life in Lancashire in a landscape that is frequently the backdrop for her poems. Her latest book is 'A Box of Silver Birch' (1997) from which the last two poems in this selection are taken. In previous years she has produced 14 other collections of her own poetry; selections from these books are most easily available in 'The Leave Train, New and Selected Poems' (Enitharmon, 1994).

The poems chosen here to represent her work fall into several groups. We begin with a portrait which explores the mixture of laughter and sadness we all feel from time to time and which is caught in the figure of the clown. The next poem is about a child who does not fit in comfortably to the world of school. Then follows a group of animal poems, each one very different in tone as the words capture what is special about the particular creature. We move from the soft, gentle world of the spotted fawn ('The First Day'), to the 'jewelled torpedo' ('The Kingfisher'), to 'the owl's clock-face without fingers' ('Owl') and, finally, to a more general poem which sums up the contradictory nature of one of our most common domestic pets ('Cats'). This selection ends with two poems which, in their different ways, express the feelings of the writer, now nearing 90 years old, about aspects of the present-day world. 'Fairy Story' is a way of writing about the breakdown in family life. 'Remembrance Day' looks back across the century to the writer's childhood and frames these memories within some opening and closing lines about the ceremony that takes place every year on November 11th.

CLOWN

He was safe
behind the whitened face
and red nose of his trade,
vocation more certain
than doctor's or priest's
to cheer and heal.
Hidden away from himself
he could always make us laugh
turning troubles like jackets
inside out, wearing
our rents and patches.
Tripping up in trousers too long
he made us feel tall;
and when we watched him
cutting himself down,
missing the ball,
we knew we could cope.

What we never knew
was the tightrope he walked
when the laughter had died.
Nowhere to hide in the empty night,
no one to catch his fall.

SALLY

She was a dog-rose kind of girl:
Elusive, scattery as petals;
Scratchy sometimes, tripping you like briars.
She teased the boys
Turning this way and that, not to be tamed
Or taught any more than the wind.
Even in school the word 'ought' had no meaning
For Sally. On dull days
She'd sit quiet as a mole at her desk
Delving in thought.
But when the sun called
She was gone, running the blue day down
Till the warm hedgerows prickled the dusk
And moths flickered out.

Her mother scolded; Dad
Gave her the hazel switch,
Said her head was stuffed with feathers
And a starling tongue.
But they couldn't take the shine out of her,
Even when it rained
You felt the sun saved under her skin.
She'd a way of escape
Laughing at you from the bright end of a tunnel,
Leaving you in the dark.

OWL

The owl's a clock-face without fingers,
two keyholes for seeing,
striking silent as frost.

Soft, unexpected as snow,
its flight a wash
through trees without flicker of leaf,
a pocket of air
bulging with warm swallowed blood.

Out there the wood grown stiller
than winter with spring breathing blue-
bells and fern under cover;
each feather pinned; fur and whisker
twitching in windless night.
And Time flying white from the clock-tower
screeching the hour of death.

THE FIRST DAY

The spotted fawn
Awoke in small leaf-spotted suns
That quivered on his tawny back
Tattooing him with coins where he lay
Beside his mother's warmth the first day
That gave him light.
The day that played him tunes
In water-music twinkling over stones
And leaf-edged undertones.
The day he learned the feel
Of dew on grass
Cool, cool and wet,
Of sun that steals the dew with sudden heat,
And heard the fret
In wind-turned willow leaves and wrinkled pool.
The day that filled his breath with pollened wind
And smell of bracken, earth, and dell-deep moss,
The day he came to know
Sharp hunger and the flow
Of milk to comfort his small emptiness,
The strangeness of his legs,
The bulwark of his mother's side,
The solace of her pink tongue's first caress,
Her snow-soft belly for his sheltering,
The rhythm of untaught desires
For movement and for rest,
For food and warmth and nest
Of flattened grass to fold himself in sleep.

KINGFISHER

Brown as nettle-beer, the stream
Shadow-freckled, specked with sun
Slides between the trees.

Not a ripple breaks in foam;
Only the frilled hedge-parsley falls
White upon the ground.
No insect drills the air; no sound
Rustles among the reeds.
Bird and leaf and thought are still
When shot from the blue a kingfisher
Flashes between the ferns —
Jewelled torpedo sparkling by
Under the bridge and gone —
Yet bright as a bead behind the eye,
The image blazes on.

CATS

Cats are contradictions: tooth and claw
Velvet-padded;
Snowflake-gentle paw
A fist of pins;
Kettles on the purr
Ready to spit;
Black silk then bristled fur.

Cats are of the East —
Scimitar and sphinx;
Sunlight striped with shade.
Leopard, lion, lynx
Moss-footed in a frightened glade;
Slit eyes an amber glint
Or boring through the darkness cool as jade.

Cats have come to rest
Upon the cushioned West.
Here, dyed-in-the-silk,
They lap up bottled milk
But must return
To the mottled woods of spring
Making the trees afraid
With leaf and wing
A-flutter at the movement in the fern.

Midnight-wild with phosphorescent eyes
Cats are morning-wise
Sleeping as they stare into the sun,
Blind to the light,
Deaf to echoing cries
From a ravaged wood;
Cats are black and white rolled into one.

FAIRY STORY

I spent the first month peeling onions
explaining my tears to my daughter.
How was she to know
what I felt that breakfast
he took a suitcase
with his briefcase
and, without the customary kiss,
closed the door on us?

I was a shot pigeon
trailing my wings, grounded
by children's needs
for food and bedtime stories.

'Don't cry,' said the eldest,
'It's not true; the prince is pretending.'
But the middle one laughed:
'Don't forget the Good Fairy!'
Puzzled, the youngest looked up:
'Father Christmas needs a year
to fill his sack.
He's promised me a polar bear
when he comes back.'

REMEMBRANCE DAY

Armistice Day, November 1918

On the eleventh day of the eleventh month
the clock strikes . . .
All I remember is being given an orange.
I was nine years old and at boarding school.

We hadn't tasted oranges for four years
or bananas or butter and eggs;
everything was grey, like the bread, and cold
like today.

It began for me
when my father went away,
and mother cried.
When he came home on leave
my sister and I
hid under the table, terrified
of the khaki stranger whose belt
shone, like a horse-chestnut.
And terrified
of the Thing, like a huge cigar,
silent, sliding over the Ribble★.   ★a river in Lancashire
They called it a zeppelin★.   ★an airship

My father stayed on
in the desert, and mother cried
all through Christmas and into the spring.
I remember the day
we felt hungry; my sister stole sugar;
I took the salt.
Now, none of you remember
what the poppies and the Last Post
mean to us . . .

R S THOMAS 1913–

R S Thomas was born in Cardiff and brought up and educated in Holyhead. His parents were not Welsh-speaking, but while he was a student in Bangor, he determined to learn Welsh. This became even more important to him during his training to be a priest, for many of his future parishioners in rural North Wales would be Welsh speakers. Perhaps the key to understanding his poems lies in his remark that 'the necessary qualifications of a truly Anglo-Welsh writer (are) that he should steep himself in all things Welsh to justify the hyphen'. That hyphen, for R S Thomas, is an uncomfortable, permanent reminder of his divided self. For, while he has immersed himself in the Welsh language and culture, he has only been able to write poetry in his mother tongue: making poems demands an instinctive way with words that he cannot achieve in a second language. This dilemma runs through all his work and means that he shares some of the mixed feelings about nationality and language that are found in other hyphenated groups of writers, the Afro-Caribbean, or the West Indian-British poets such as John Agard (pp. 210–216).

The other theme throughout his poetry is religious. He was a parish priest in the Anglican Church for the whole of his working life until he retired in 1978. His ministry brought him closely in touch with the poor rural communities of North Wales and, along with his admiration and sympathy for the ordinary people, there is often a bitter feeling about their living conditions. In one poem he portrays himself as waiting 'somewhere between faith and doubt'. While his beliefs are unshakeable, as 'The Coming' (p. 196) indicates, his poems suggest that he found the practice of his ministry was often a challenge to those beliefs.

The selection here begins with a dialogue between two poets arguing about the best way to write and ends with his well-known 'Welsh Landscape' (p. 196) which sums up all the mixed feelings of love, frustration and bitterness he has at the history, landscape and language of Wales. In between, there are poems about childhood and about some of the characters from the hard rural country that Thomas knows so well.

POETRY FOR SUPPER

'Listen, now, verse should be as natural
As the small tuber that feeds on muck
And grows slowly from obtuse soil
To the white flower of immortal beauty.'

'Natural, hell! What was it Chaucer
Said once about the long toil
That goes like blood to the poem's making?
Leave it to nature and the verse sprawls,
Limp as bindweed, if it break at all
Life's iron crust. Man, you must sweat
And rhyme your guts taut, if you'd build
Your verse a ladder.'
                         'You speak as though
No sunlight ever surprised the mind
Groping on its cloudy path.'

'Sunlight's a thing that needs a window
Before it enter a dark room.
Windows don't happen.'

                    So two old poets,
Hunched at their beer in the low haze
Of an inn parlour, while the talk ran
Noisily by them, glib with prose.

CYNDDYLAN ON A TRACTOR

Ah, you should see Cynddylan on a tractor.
Gone the old look that yoked him to the soil;
He's a new man now, part of the machine.
His nerves of metal and his blood oil.
The clutch curses, but the gears obey
His least bidding, and lo, he's away
Out of the farmyard, scattering hens.
Riding to work now as a great man should,
He is the knight at arms breaking the fields'
Mirror of silence, emptying the wood
Of foxes and squirrels and bright jays.
The sun comes over the tall trees
Kindling all the hedges, but not for him
Who runs his engine on a different fuel.
And all the birds are singing, bills wide in vain,
As Cynddylan passed proudly up the lane.

THE HILL FARMER SPEAKS

I am the farmer, stripped of love
And thought and grace by the land's hardness;
But what I am saying over the fields'
Desolate acres, rough with dew,
Is, Listen, listen, I am a man like you.

The wind goes over the hill pastures
Year after year, and the ewes starve,
Milkless, for want of the new grass.
And I starve, too, for something the spring
Can never foster in veins run dry.

The pig is a friend, the cattle's breath
Mingles with mine in the still lanes;
I wear it willingly like a cloak
To shelter me from your curious gaze.

The hens go in and out at the door
From sun to shadow, as stray thoughts pass
Over the floor of my wide skull.
The dirt is under my cracked nails;
The tale of my life is smirched with dung;
The phlegm rattles. But what I am saying
Over the grasses rough with dew
Is, Listen, listen, I am a man like you.

FARM CHILD

Look at this village boy, his head is stuffed
With all the nests he knows, his pockets with flowers,
Snail shells and bits of glass, the fruit of hours
Spent in the fields by thorn and thistle tuft.
Look at his eyes, see the harebell hiding there;
Mark how the sun has freckled his smooth face
Like a finch's egg under that bush of hair
That dares the wind, and in the mixen* now   *dunghill
Notice his poise; from such unconscious grace
Earth breeds and beckons to the stubborn plough.

CHILDREN'S SONG

We live in our own world,
A world that is too small
For you to stoop and enter
Even on hands and knees,
The adult subterfuge.
And though you probe and pry
With analytic eye,
And eavesdrop all our talk
With an amused look,
You cannot find the centre
Where we dance, where we play,
Where life is still asleep
Under the closed flower,
Under the smooth shell
Of eggs in the cupped nest
That mock the faded blue
Of your remoter heaven.

THE COMING

And God held in his hand
A small globe. Look, he said.
The son looked. Far off
As through water, he saw
A scorched land of fierce
Colour. The light burned
There; crusted buildings
Cast their shadows; a bright
Serpent, a river
Uncoiled itself, radiant
With slime.
        On a bare
Hill a bare tree saddened
The sky. Many people
Held out their thin arms
To it, as though waiting
For a vanished April
To return to its crossed
Boughs. The son watched
Them. Let me go there, he said.

WELSH LANDSCAPE

To live in Wales is to be conscious
At dusk of the spilled blood
That went to the making of the wild sky,
Dyeing the immaculate rivers
In all their courses.
It is to be aware,
Above the noisy tractor
And hum of the machine
Of strife in the strung woods,
Vibrant with sped arrows.
You cannot live in the present,
At least not in Wales.
There is the language for instance,
The soft consonants
Strange to the ear.
There are cries in the dark at night
As owls answer the moon,
And thick ambush of shadows,
Hushed at the fields' corners.
There is no present in Wales,
And no future;
There is only the past,
Brittle with relics,
Wind-bitten towers and castles
With sham ghosts;
Mouldering quarries and mines;
And an impotent people,
Sick with inbreeding,
Worrying the carcase of an old song.

U A FANTHORPE, 1929-

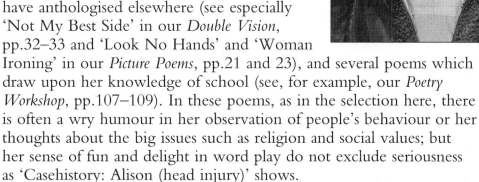

U A Fanthorpe has described herself as 'a middle-aged drop-out'. She was born in London, educated at Oxford and then taught at Cheltenham Ladies' College where she became Head of the English Department. Her first volume of poems did not appear until 1978. Since then, she has devoted more of her time to writing. Her most recent books are 'Neck Verse' (1992) and 'Safe as Houses' (1995) both published by the Peterloo Press. Selections from her earlier books are most conveniently found in her 'Selected Poems' (Penguin, 1986).

Her subjects range widely so that it is difficult here to do justice to the variety of her poetry. She has written some memorable poems in response to paintings which we have anthologised elsewhere (see especially 'Not My Best Side' in our *Double Vision*, pp.32–33 and 'Look No Hands' and 'Woman Ironing' in our *Picture Poems*, pp.21 and 23), and several poems which draw upon her knowledge of school (see, for example, our *Poetry Workshop*, pp.107–109). In these poems, as in the selection here, there is often a wry humour in her observation of people's behaviour or her thoughts about the big issues such as religion and social values; but her sense of fun and delight in word play do not exclude seriousness as 'Casehistory: Alison (head injury)' shows.

U A Fanthorpe often takes 'a sideways look' at life, writing about her subject from an unfamiliar angle and making us, her readers, look at it afresh. We see the Nativity from the point of view of one of the shepherds' dogs or from that of a cat who claims to have been there (p. 202). We eavesdrop on the conversations of holiday-makers who fly off to different resorts ('First Flight' and 'Travelling Man'). We hear the echoes of 'Old Macdonald had a farm' and 'Uncle Tom Cobley' in a soap opera poem about the Monarchy. In these, as in all her poems, U A Fanthorpe is a sympathetic observer of the way we live as well as being thought-provoking, witty and unstuffy in the way she writes.

FIRST FLIGHT

Plane moves. I don't like the feel of it.
In a car I'd suspect low tyre pressure.

A sudden swiftness, earth slithers
Off at an angle. The experienced solidly

    This is rather a short hop for me

Read *Guardians*, discuss secretaries,
Business lunches. I crane for the last of dear

    I'm doing it just to say I've done it

Familiar England, motorways, reservoir,
Building sites. Nimble tiny disc, a sun

    Tell us when we get to water

Runs up the porthole and vanishes,
Under us the broad meringue kingdom

    The next lot of water'll be the Med

Of cumulus, bearing the crinkled tangerine stain
That light spreads on an evening sea at home.

    You don't need an overcoat, but
    It's the sort of place where you need
    A pullover. Know what I mean?

We have come too high for history.
Where we are now deals only with tomorrow,
Confounds the forecasters, dismisses clocks.

    My last trip was Beijing. Know where that is?
    Beijing. Peking, you'd say. Three weeks there, I was.
    Peking is wrong. If you've been there
    You call it Beijing, like me. Go on, say it.

Mackerel wigs dispense the justice of air.
At this height nothing lives. Too cold. Too near the sun.

TRAVELLING MAN

Wonderful where you can go nowadays
(He says). Where you can go,
What you can learn. It wer Portugal
This year for us (he says).

Now the wife, she gets a bit bored like
Wi' culture. But me,
I wanted to see Wellington's campaign
Int' flesh, you might say.

'Course, being a package tour, we only
Went where they took us.
But magic places, magic. Porto, now,
And Jerez. I liked Jerez.

Last year it wer Italy. Vesuvius
(All that lava, y'know) and Pompey,
And Rome. Wonderful, wonderful!
And Sorrento. What a name!

I couldn't lie about on beaches
(He says). I like to see t'sights.
But I feel guilty about th'owd uns.
They din't ave these chances.

Me grandparents, y'know. I feel guilty
They din't see this,
They din't gerrabout. Me grandmother,
When she cum from Blackpool to see us,

She allus said *I ave to be ome at night*
To get t'meat (cheap cuts, that were, y'know).
She wouldn't ave wanted. And me mother,
She just laughs at me feelin guilty.

She says *Your father ud never*
Sleep in a strange bed.

CASEHISTORY: ALISON (HEAD INJURY)

(*She looks at her photograph*)

I would like to have known
My husband's wife, my mother's only daughter.
A bright girl she was.

Enmeshed in comforting
Fat, I wonder at her delicate angles.
Her autocratic knee

Like a Degas dancer's
Adjusts to the observer with airy poise,
That now lugs me upstairs

Hardly. Her face, broken
By nothing sharper than smiles, holds in its smiles
What I have forgotten.

She knows my father's dead,
And grieves for it, and smiles. She has digested
Mourning. Her smile shows it.

I, who need reminding
Every morning, shall never get over what
I do not remember.

Consistency matters.
I should like to keep faith with her lack of faith,
But forget her reasons.

Proud of this younger self,
I assert her achievements, her A levels,
Her job with a future.

Poor clever girl! I know,
For all my damaged brain, something she doesn't:
I am her future.

A bright girl she was.

THE WINDSORS: AN EVERYDAY STORY OF ROYAL FOLK

Some people honestly believe in them,
Think they're alive, write to them, send them flowers,
Are always knitting for the newest one,
Keep albums crammed with snaps of what they've done,
Wave flags in rainswept streets for hours and hours,
    With a Grundy here and a Gloucester there,
      Here a chukka, there a chicken, here and there a corgi.
          Mrs Windsor has a realm;
          God save gracious Dan!

Some people need another family
A touch more charismatic than their own,
Glossy at Goodwood, funny at a fête,
Sound with a tractor or the Ship of State,
Despite zoom lenses goggling at their throne,
    At Prince Andrew, Shula Archer, Mrs Simpson, Mrs Perkins,
      Walter Gabriel, Princess Di,
      Old Uncle Tom Forrest and all,
      Great-uncle Mountbatten and all.

Their history is ours; our parents knew
The small print of their genealogy.
They're loyal to their fans; they seldom stray;
Death changes the cast-list, but not the play,
And when we turn the switch on, there they'll be
    Doing their bit
        for
        Garter King of Arms
        BBC
        And the NFU
        With a crown in the family tree.

THE SHEEPDOG

After the very bright light,
And the talking bird,
And the singing,
And the sky filled up wi' wings,
And then the silence,

Our lads sez
We'd better go, then.
Stay, Shep. Good dog, stay.
So I stayed wi' t' sheep.

After they cum back,
It sounded grand, what they'd seen:
Camels, and kings, and such,
Wi' presents – human sort,
Not the kind you eat –
And a baby. Presents wes for him.
Our lads took him a lamb.

I had to stay behind wi' t' sheep.
Pity they didn't tek me along too.
I'm good wi' lambs,
And the baby might have liked a dog
After all that myrrh and such.

CAT IN THE MANGER

In the story, I'm not there.
Ox and ass, arranged at prayer:
But me? Nowhere.

Anti-cat evangelists
How on earth could you have missed
Such an obvious and able
Occupant of any stable?

Who excluded mouse and rat?
The harmless necessary cat.
Who snuggled in with the holy pair?
Me. And my purr.

Matthew, Mark and Luke and John
(Who got it wrong,
Who left out the cat)
Remember that,
Wherever He went in this great affair,
I was there.

CHRISTMAS SOUNDS

Boeings wing softly over Earth
Humming like enormous *Messiahs*,
Bringing everyone home for Christmas.

Children wailing impossible wants,
Housewives worrying in case enough isn't,
Parsons, with prevenient care, sucking Strepsils,

Telly jingling twinkling mistletoe-ing,
Cash tills recording glad tidings of profit,
Office parties munching through menus —

Crackers! Champagne corks!

At the heart of it all, in the hay,
No sound at all but the cattle
Endlessly chewing it over.

BC:AD

This was the moment when Before
Turned into After, and the future's
Uninvented timekeepers presented arms.

This was the moment when nothing
Happened. Only dull peace
Sprawled boringly over the earth.

This was the moment when even energetic Romans
Could find nothing better to do
Than counting heads in remote provinces.

And this was the moment
When a few farm workers and three
Members of an obscure Persian sect

Walked haphazardly by starlight straight
Into the kingdom of heaven.

TED HUGHES, 1930–

Ted Hughes' first collection of poems 'The Hawk in the Rain' was published in 1957. Other volumes followed in steady succession. Some of them were for the general reader but others, for example, 'Season Songs' and 'Under the North Star', were written for children. The huge success, particularly of his poems about animals, led to his being created Poet Laureate in 1984.

The son of a carpenter from Mytholmroyd in Yorkshire, he spent much of his young life in and around the mining town of Mexborough. His parents moved there when he was seven to run a newsagent's and tobacconist's shop. Though it was a mining town, Hughes had easy access to the nearby countryside and to its wildlife. He was no stranger to fishing, to the ways of poachers, gamekeepers and local farmers and, of course, to the lives of the animals. He even tried on more than one occasion to capture fox cubs in order to rear them but was prevented by farmers who saw to it that they were killed before he could do so.

When Hughes was about 15 his attitude to animals changed. He said that he began to accuse himself of disturbing their lives and to look at them from their own point of view. And it was about then that he began to write poems.

He won a scholarship to Pembroke College Cambridge but first went on to complete his National Service in the RAF. He worked at a number of jobs – gardener, night watchman, zookeeper, scriptwriter and teacher before marrying the American poet Sylvia Plath in 1956. It was a difficult and often unhappy relationship which ended in his wife's suicide in 1963. This, and later tragedies were to overshadow his life and work. His most recent collection of poems 'Birthday Letters' (1998) was written over a period of 25 years after Sylvia Plath's death and almost all the poems are addressed to her.

Hughes is perhaps best known for his powerful, carefully observed poems about animals and the natural world. They are never cosy or sentimental poems: often they celebrate the raw and elemental energy of nature. In 'To Paint a Water Lily' Hughes points to the contrast between the seeming beauty of the lily above the surface 'whatever horror nudge her root'. In 'October Dawn' a glass of wine left out is found with a skim of ice on its surface next morning which to Hughes suggests the return of the ice age. His view of nature can be both bleak and harsh, reflecting the battle for survival which underlies all of nature.

But Hughes can also be tender as in 'Full Moon and Little Frieda' and humorous as in so many of his poems (and stories) written for children. His enormous and varied output can only be represented by a few poems in this selection. The one thing that unites them all is Hughes' delight in language, his ability to choose the right image to create a picture in our mind's eye and his ear for the rhythm and the life of words.

OCTOBER DAWN

October is marigold, and yet
A glass half full of wine left out

To the dark heaven all night, by dawn
Has dreamed a premonition

Of ice across its eye as if
The ice-age had begun its heave.

The lawn overtrodden and strewn
From the night before, and the whistling green

Shrubbery are doomed. Ice
Has got its spearhead into place.

First a skin, delicately here
Restraining a ripple from the air;

Soon plate and rivet upon pond and brook;
Then tons of chain and massive lock

To hold rivers. Then, sound by sight
Will Mammoth and Sabre-tooth celebrate

Reunion while a fist of cold
Squeezes the fire at the core of the world,

Squeezes the fire at the core of the heart,
And now it is about to start.

TO PAINT A WATER LILY

A green level of lily leaves
Roofs the pond's chamber and paves

The flies' furious arena: study
These, the two minds of this lady.

First observe the air's dragonfly
That eats meat, that bullets by

Or stands in space to take aim;
Others as dangerous comb the hum

Under the trees. There are battle-shouts
And death-cries everywhere hereabouts

But inaudible, so the eyes praise
To see the colours of these flies

Rainbow their arcs, spark, or settle
Cooling like beads of molten metal

Through the spectrum. Think what worse
Is the pond-bed's matter of course;

Prehistoric bedragonned times
Crawl that darkness with Latin names,

Have evolved no improvements there,
Jaws for heads, the set stare,

Ignorant of age as of hour—
Now paint the long-necked lily-flower

Which, deep in both worlds, can be still
As a painting, trembling hardly at all

Though the dragonfly alight,
Whatever horror nudge her root.

THE WARM AND THE COLD

Freezing dusk is closing
  Like a slow trap of steel
On trees and roads and hills and all
  That can no longer feel.
      But the carp is in its depth
        Like a planet in its heaven.
      And the badger in its bedding
        Like a loaf in the oven.
      And the butterfly in its mummy
        Like a viol in its case.
      And the owl in its feathers
        Like a doll in its lace.

Freezing dusk has tightened
  Like a nut screwed tight
On the starry aeroplane
  Of the soaring night.
      But the trout is in its hole
        Like a chuckle in a sleeper.
      The hare strays down the highway
        Like a root going deeper.
      The snail is dry in the outhouse
        Like a seed in a sunflower.
      The owl is pale on the gatepost
        Like a clock on its tower.

Moonlight freezes the shaggy world
  Like a mammoth of ice—
The past and the future
  Are the jaws of a steel vice.
      But the cod is in the tide-rip
        Like a key in a purse.
      The deer are on the bare-blown hill
        Like smiles on a nurse.
      The flies are behind the plaster
        Like the lost score of a jig.
      Sparrows are in the ivy-clump
        Like money in a pig.

Such a frost
  The flimsy moon
    Has lost her wits.

          A star falls.

The sweating farmers
  Turn in their sleep
    Like oxen on spits.

SNOWDROP

Now is the globe shrunk tight
Round the mouse's dulled wintering heart.
Weasel and crow, as if moulded in brass,
Move through an outer darkness
Not in their right minds,
With the other deaths. She, too, pursues her ends,
Brutal as the stars of this month,
Her pale head heavy as metal.

FULL MOON AND LITTLE FRIEDA

A cool small evening shrunk to a dog bark and the clank
   of a bucket –

And you listening.
A spider's web, tense for the dew's touch.
A pail lifted, still and brimming – mirror
To tempt a first star to a tremor.

Cows are going home in the lane there, looping the
   hedges with their warm wreaths of breath –
A dark river of blood, many boulders,
Balancing unspilled milk.

'Moon!' you cry suddenly, 'Moon! Moon!'

The moon has stepped back like an artist gazing amazed
   at a work

That points at him amazed.

MOOSES

The goofy Moose, the walking house-frame,
Is lost
In the forest. He bumps, he blunders, he stands.

With massy bony thoughts sticking out near his ears—
Reaching out palm upwards, to catch whatever might be
   falling from heaven—
He tries to think,
Leaning their huge weight
On the lectern of his front legs.

He can't find the world!
Where did it go? What does a world look like?
The Moose
Crashes on, and crashes into a lake, and stares at the
   mountain, and cries
'Where do I belong? This is no place!'

He turns and drags half the lake out after him
And charges the cackling underbrush—

He meets another Moose.
He stares, he thinks 'It's only a mirror!'

'Where is the world?' he groans, 'O my lost world!
And why am I so ugly?
And why am I so far away from my feet?'

He weeps.
Hopeless drops drip from his droopy lips.

The other Moose just stands there doing the same.

Two dopes of the deep woods.

THE JAGUAR

The apes yawn and adore their fleas in the sun.
The parrots shriek as if they were on fire, or strut
Like cheap tarts to attract the stroller with the nut.
Fatigued with indolence, tiger and lion

Lie still as the sun. The boa-constrictor's coil
Is a fossil. Cage after cage seems empty, or
Stinks of sleepers from the breathing straw.
It might be painted on a nursery wall.

But who runs like the rest past these arrives
At a cage where the crowd stands, stares, mesmerized,
As a child at a dream, at a jaguar hurrying enraged
Through prison darkness after the drills of his eyes

On a short fierce fuse. Not in boredom –
The eye satisfied to be blind in fire,
By the bang of blood in the brain deaf the ear –
He spins from the bars, but there's no cage to him

More than to the visionary his cell:
His stride is wildernesses of freedom:
The world rolls under the long thrust of his heel.
Over the cage floor the horizons come.

JOHN AGARD, 1949–

'So come on everybody
join de celebration ...'

In John Agard's poems words dance
to a different tune from those of the
other poets in this section. His poems
need to be spoken and performed; they
have their own music, often with
echoes of the steel bands and calypsoes
of his homeland in the Caribbean.
Their words are alive with the
everyday rhythms of West Indian
speech. These poems are like
invitations to get in the party mood – a
'poetry jump-up'; but, while the sense of fun is everywhere, there is
also a sharp point to many of his poems, not least about the difficulties
of black people living in a mainly white society.

John Agard was born in British Guiana (now Guyana). In 1977
he came to England and worked for the Commonwealth Institute for
some years as a touring speaker giving readings, talks and workshops
on Caribbean culture and poetry. He is now a freelance writer and
performer of poetry for both adults and children and appears
frequently on radio and television. In 1993 he became the first Writer
in Residence at London's South Bank Centre; and in 1998 he was
appointed the first Poet in Residence at the BBC. He has published
many volumes of his own verse and edited several anthologies. The
two books we have drawn upon most for this selection are 'Mangoes
and Bullets' (Serpent's Tail, 1985) and 'Get Back Pimple' (Puffin,
1997). We begin with a group of light-hearted poems from this
second collection, written with young readers in mind; we finish with
two poems ('Half-Caste' and 'Stereotype') which draw the reader in
with the same humour and then, by the end, make the reader think
about the serious point behind the words. As you may have seen in
his poem 'Rainbow' (p. 11), John Agard's poems often produce a
'thoughtful smile' when we read them.

POETRY JUMP-UP

Tell me if Ah seeing right
Take a look down de street

Words dancin
words dancin
till dey sweat
words like fishes
jumpin out a net
words wild and free
joinin de poetry revelry
words back to back
words belly to belly

Come on everybody
come and join de poetry band
dis is poetry carnival
dis is poetry bacchanal
when inspiration call
take yu pen in yu hand
if yu don't have a pen
take yu pencil in yu hand
if yu don't have a pencil
what the hell
so long de feeling start to swell
just shout de poem out

Words jumpin off de page
tell me if Ah seein right
words like birds
jumping out a cage
take a look down de street
words shakin dey waist
words shakin dey bum
words wit black skin
words wit white skin
words wit brown skin
words wit no skin at all
words huggin up words
an sayin I want to be a poem today
rhyme or no rhyme
I is a poem today
I mean to have a good time

Words feeling hot hot hot
big words feeling hot hot hot
lil words feeling hot hot hot
even sad words cant help
tappin dey toe
to de riddum of de poetry band

Dis is poetry carnival
dis is poetry bacchanal
so come on everybody
join de celebration
all yu need is plenty perspiration
an a little inspiration
plenty perspiration
an a little inspiration

NOT-ENOUGH-POCKET-MONEY BLUES

I could see myself stepping light and slow
in them jeans
so hip-sharp-tight and full-of-flow.
Could just
But I've got me the no-cash no-dosh
not-enough-pocket-money blues.

Could see myself slinking to school
in them trainers
so jaguar-sleek and puma-cool.
Could just …
But I've got me the no-cash no-dosh
not-enough-pocket-money blues.

Could see myself a fashion queen
in that top
so flirty-smart and snazzy-sleeved.
Could just …
But I've got me the no-cash no-dosh
not-enough-pocket-money blues.

Could see myself all summery
in that hat
so patchwork-wicked and flowery.
Could just …
But I've got me the no-cash no-dosh
not-enough-pocket-money blues.

I guess I can always ask Mum.

SPELL TO BANISH A PIMPLE

Get back pimple
get back to where you belong

Get back to never-never land
and I hope you stay there long

Get back pimple
get back to where you belong

How dare you take residence
in the middle of my face

I never offered you a place
beside my dimple

Get back pimple
get back to where you belong

Get packing pimple
I banish you to outer space

If only life was that simple

SMOKE-LOVING GIRL BLUES

Would like her for my girlfriend any day
Would follow if she showed the way
Would feel honoured if she be my queen

But she's a smoke-loving girl
And I'm allergic to nicotine

Would wheel with her on the ice-skating rink
Would fall with her over the brink
Would stare with her bewitched and serene

But she's a smoke-loving girl
And I'm allergic to nicotine

Would give her my last polo mint
Would hit the skies if she gave me a hint
Would do anything even dye my hair green

But she's a smoke-loving girl
And I'm allergic to nicotine

Would lay down my jacket for her gorgeous feet
Would fan her cheeks to keep away the heat
Would shine her shoes till she's lost in the sheen

But she's a smoke-loving girl
And I'm allergic to nicotine

Lawd now my head is in a haze
Cause of that girl and her smoke-loving ways

A DATE WITH SPRING

Got a date with Spring
Got to look me best.
Of all the trees
I'll be the smartest dressed.

Perfumed breeze
behind me ear.
Pollen accessories
all in place.
Raindrop moisturizer
for me face.
Sunlight tints
to spruce up the hair.

What's the good of being a tree
if you can't flaunt your beauty?

Winter, I was naked.
Exposed as can be.
Me wardrobe took off
with the wind.
Life was a frosty slumber
Now, Spring, here I come
Can't wait to slip in
to me little green number.

CHILD WAITING

(for lesley)

little head
at the window
in childeyed wonder

the ceaseless
come and go
of mighty traffic
must be moving magic
to your unblinking gaze

but how patient
are eyes looking for one
named mummy
in a rumble of wheels

HALF-CASTE

Excuse me
standing on one leg
I'm half-caste

Explain yuself
wha yu mean
when yu say half-caste
yu mean when picasso
mix red an green
is a half-caste canvas/
explain yuself
wha yu mean
when yu say half-caste
yu mean when light an shadow
mix in de sky
is a half-caste weather/
well in dat case
england weather
nearly always half-caste
in fact some o dem cloud
half-caste till dem overcast
so spiteful dem dont want de sun pass
ah rass/
explain yuself
wha yu mean
when yu say half-caste
yu mean when tchaikovsky
sit down at dah piano
an mix a black key
wid a white key
is a half-caste symphony/

Explain yuself
wha yu mean
Ah listening to yu wid de keen
half of mih ear
Ah lookin at yu wid de keen
half of mih eye
an when I'm introduced to you
I'm sure you'll understand
why I offer yu half-a-hand
an when I sleep at night
I close half-a-eye
consequently when I dream
I dream half-a-dream
an when moon begin to glow
I half-caste human being
cast half-a-shadow
but yu must come back tomorrow

wid de whole of yu eye
an de whole of yu ear
an de whole of yu mind

an I will tell yu
de other half
of my story

STEREOTYPE

I'm a fullblooded
West Indian stereotype
See me straw hat?
Watch it good

I'm a fullblooded
West Indian stereotype
You ask
if I got riddum
in me blood
You going ask!
Man just beat de drum
and don't forget
to pour de rum

I'm a fullblooded
West Indian stereotype
You say
I suppose you can show
us the limbo, can't you?
How you know!
How you know!
You sure
you don't want me
sing you a calypso too
How about that

I'm a fullblooded
West Indian stereotype
You call me
happy-go-lucky
Yes that's me
dressing fancy
and chasing woman
if you think ah lie
bring yuh sister

I'm a fullblooded
West Indian stereotype
You wonder
where do you people
get such riddum
could it be the sunshine
My goodness
just listen to that steelband

Isn't there one thing
you forgot to ask
go on man ask ask
This native will answer anything
How about cricket?
I suppose you're good at it?
Hear this man
good at it!
Put de willow
in me hand
and watch me stripe
de boundary

Yes I'm a fullblooded
West Indian stereotype

that's why I
graduated from Oxford University
with a degree
in anthropology

Ten Poets Workshop

Below are a few ideas for work on these poets. In particular, you will be able to follow up on any writer who appeals to you by getting the listed book from the library and asking for guidance from your teacher.

(1) Reading and Activities

Chaucer: *The General Prologue to the Canterbury Tales*, ed. A C Spearing, CUP.

- Have a look at one or two of the other character portraits from this General Prologue, for example, the Knight and the Squire. Try to write a few lines of your own in Chaucerian English, perhaps describing one of your friends. To give you the idea, here is how one student began his portrait of a school teacher:

  > 'The Schole-maistere'
  > Ther was with us a lerned Schole-maistere
  > That was on toppe as bald as is a frere...

Tennyson: *The Lady of Shalott*, illustrated by Charles Keeping, OUP.

- This poem has been illustrated many times. Try to look at this modern edition and also at two famous paintings from the last century by J Waterhouse and Holman Hunt, both of which are reproduced in colour in our *Double Vision* (Hodder & Stoughton). Which pictures do you prefer and why?

Clare: *John Clare*, ed. E. Robinson and D. Powell, OUP.

- Make a wall display of a selection of Clare's poems on animals and the natural world. Include poems which give a clear word-picture. Add your own illustrations.

Dickinson: *A Choice of Emily Dickinson's Verse*, ed. Ted Hughes, Faber & Faber.

- Emily Dickinson's poems look very closely at the objects they describe. Try to do the same. Choose a particular object, maybe one that you have collected on holiday (a pebble, a shell, driftwood?), and list all the details you notice. Find words for its shape, colour, texture, and any thoughts and feelings it brings back to you. Write up your notes into a poem.

Lawrence: *Selected Poems*, ed. W E Williams, Penguin.

- Look at the poem 'Bat' (p. 184) and see how Lawrence arranges his ideas and phrases. Notice what he does and does not do. He does not bother with rhyme; he varies the length of his lines; and he uses comparisons. Discuss with your teacher why Lawrence chooses to do each of these things. Now, write your own poem about an animal in the same style.

Hesketh: *The Leave Train. New and Selected Poems*, Enitharmon Press.

- In the introduction to Phoebe Hesketh (p. 188) we have picked out several phrases from the group of four animal poems. Choose two or three different creatures and write down a phrase of your own which catches the movement or appearance of each one. Develop your phrases into haiku poems (see Unit 1, pp. 3–4).

Thomas: *Collected Poems 1945–1990*, J M Dent.

- Read the poem 'The Coming' (p. 196) and talk about it with your teacher. God and his son look into the 'small globe' as though gazing into a crystal ball. In the first part, what do they see? In the second part, when the son sees the 'bare tree' with 'crossed boughs', why does he want to go there?

Fanthorpe: *Selected Poems*, Penguin.

- Read the poems 'Cat in the Manger' and 'The Sheepdog' (p. 202) and talk about them with your teacher. Write a description of the Nativity from another animal's point of view.

Hughes: *Season Songs* and *Under the North Star*, Faber & Faber.

- Read the poem 'To Paint a Water Lily' (p. 206) and discuss it with your teacher. What is seen on the surface of the pond? What lies below? At the end of the poem, what is it that interests Hughes about the water lily? Write a sequel to this poem, making your own word-picture of, say, a willow tree, bullrushes, or a swan. Paint the beautiful surface appearance and then imagine what is just below....

Agard: *Get Back Pimple*, Puffin.

- In groups, choose three or four poems and rehearse a performance to give to the rest of the class.

(2) Poetry Contest

The idea here is rather like the Eurovision Song Contest – in this case to find out which group can perform the best poetry presentation.

In groups (10 groups, one per poet)

For the purposes of the contest, each group adopts one of the poets, reads through his or her work and lists the reasons why this particular writer should win.

To prepare your presentation:
- decide which are the two or three best poems by your poet;
- rehearse readings of your chosen poems to perform to the class;
- prepare a brief list of points saying why this writer is good and what your audience should look out for;
- give your presentation.

Marking:
- each group gives a mark out of 10 for each presentation (max. score: 90).
- in deciding your mark, take into account the quality of the readings and the reasons given for why the writer should win. Remember, you are judging the presentation, not whether you like the poems or not.

(3) Autobiography

All poets write about themselves, directly or indirectly, but there are some poems which very clearly reflect the feelings of the writer about some aspect of his or her life. Here are six examples from this part of the book:

John Clare	: 'Written in Northampton County Asylum'	p. 162
Alfred, Lord Tennyson	: 'Crossing the Bar'	p. 174
D H Lawrence	: 'Last Lesson of the Afternoon'	p. 183
Phoebe Hesketh	: 'Remembrance Day'	p. 192
R S Thomas	: 'Welsh Landscape'	p. 196
John Agard	: 'Child Waiting'	p. 214

In pairs

- Read the six poems. You will see that the first two reveal the writers looking towards the next world rather than this one. These are quite different from Lawrence's memories of school teaching or John Agard's portrait of his daughter watching for her mother's return home.
- Choose two or three of the poems and, with your teacher, read through the Introductions to the poets so that you know when they lived and something about them.
- Compose a single sentence for each of your choices which sums up what it tells you about this aspect of the poet's life.

(4) Imaging

On your own

- Choose *one* poet whose work appeals to you, and jot down a list of words and phrases that the poems suggest to you. Include quotations from the poems, associations, memories, feelings, thoughts....

In pairs or groups

- Compare your list with those of one or two others who have been thinking about the same poet.
- Build up a wall display on 'your poet' from your combined notes. Include some suitable illustrations. Present an image of your poet in words and pictures.

Glossary of Technical Terms

There are scores of technical terms to describe different poetic structures and techniques: fortunately, it is perfectly possible to talk intelligently and sensitively about poetry using very few of them. Nonetheless, we have found it helpful to use several of them once or twice at least in the course of this book and have listed those that appear in the text along with a few others that you are likely to come across and that you may yourself find it helpful to use as you gain more confidence in talking and writing about poetry.

alliteration   (note the spelling: NOT **ill**...!) When the same consonant sound is repeated in words or syllables in close succession. It usually refers to the repetition of a sound or letter at the beginning of words, as in

> **He clasps the crag with hooked hands**

where the repetition of the *c* and *h* helps the sound to echo the meaning when we say the line aloud, but it can appear elsewhere in the line as in

> **Fields ever fresh and groves ever green**

where, apart from the repetition of *f* and *g* there is a less noticeable repetition of the letter *v*. In this book there are a number of examples of both alliteration and assonance on pp. 35–38. See also 'The Blacksmiths' (p. 38) and 'Cat' (p. 37).

assonance   The echoing of similar vowel sounds in the same line or consecutive lines. Thus *place* and *fade* are assonance. See pp. 35–38.

ballad   A narrative poem (i.e. one that tells a story) usually written in four line stanzas rhyming *abcb* or *abab*. It may have a repeated refrain (i.e. a line or verse that is repeated at certain fixed points in the poem). The language is usually simple. See the examples in Part A of this book (pp. 17–23) and on pp. 70–78 in Part B.

blank verse   Verse composed of an indefinite number of unrhymed iambic pentameters. Most of Shakespeare's plays and much of

Wordsworth's poetry are in blank verse. (See **iambic pentameter** under **rhythm**, **stress**, **metre** below.)

consonant   A speech sound which is not a vowel, for example b, c, d, f, g, h, j are consonants. Consonants are combined with a vowel to make a syllable. (See **vowel**.)

couplet   A pair of lines usually of the same metre which have a common rhyme, as in

> **True ease in writing comes from art, not chance,**
> **As those move easiest who have learned to dance.**

The lines from 'The Canterbury Tales' pp. 148–160 are all rhymed couplets.

free verse   Poetry which has no regular metre or rhyme pattern as, for example, on p. 184 'Bat'. Properly, the content and mood of the poem suggest its form or shape on the page. See also Part A, pp. 25–26.

haiku   A form of tightly structured formal Japanese poem which, in its English form, usually has seventeen syllables arranged in three lines of five, seven and five syllables. This 'rule' is often broken in translations of haiku into English where stress rather than syllable counting is more important. See pp. 3–4 for further examples.

image/imagery   Images in poetry are pictures or sense impressions conveyed in words by the writer. An image in poetry is one which has a direct appeal to one or more of our five senses and will often involve a comparison between two or more usually unrelated objects (see **simile** and **metaphor**). One can talk about the images Ted Hughes uses in 'Wind' p. 15 or about Ted Hughes's imagery. See also pp. 6–10 of Part A.

irony/ironic   Irony is when a writer suggests a meaning which might be quite different from, even opposite to, the one he or she *appears* to offer us. We may sometimes say something is ironic when the opposite of what we might have expected actually happens and causes a certain amount of amusement.

metaphor   A direct comparison of one thing with another without the introductory *like* or *as*. Ted Hughes' poem 'Work and Play' (p. 128) describes a swallow as 'a blue-dark knot of glittering voltage/a whiplash swimmer, a fish of the air' and describes a traffic jam as 'a serpent of cars'. He does not write it is *like* a knot, a swimmer, a fish, or a serpent. See also pp. 6–10 on metaphor and simile. Such comparison is at the heart of poetry and like simile it yokes together in words, and so in the images in our minds, things we had not previously connected. Louis Untermeyer wrote: 'Its element is surprise. To relate the hitherto un-related, to make the strange seem familiar and the familiar seem strange is the aim of metaphor. Through this heightened awareness, poetry, though variously defined, is invariably pronounced and unmistakably perceived.'

mood or **tone**   The prevailing state of mind or feeling of the poem which the writer appears to suggest to the reader and the overall emotional effect it generates. For example, one might speak of the sombre or lively tone or mood of the poem.

onomatopoeia   A word whose sound imitates and therefore suggests its meaning as in bow-wow, hiss, whizz, crackle, cuckoo.

parody   A piece of writing which imitates the characteristics of a writer's style or a type of poem with the intention of making fun of it. 'Alternative Endings to an Unwritten Ballad' (p. 76) is a parody of the ballad form.

pastiche   A piece of writing which imitates the characteristics of a writer's style.

personification   Giving human shape or characteristics to something non-human e.g. an animal or an inanimate object or an abstract concept such as Peace, Love, War; or addressing an inanimate object or abstract quality as though it were a person as in

> **O Moon, look down from thy silver sphere**

See also the examples of 'Despair' and 'Gluttony' on p. 12.

quatrain   A four line stanza or group of lines which may have various rhyme schemes. The commonest verse form in English.

rhyme   Identity of sound between words or verse lines in which the vowel and closing consonant sounds of a stressed syllable are repeated together with any weak syllables which may follow. In poetry, the letter or letters preceding the accented vowel must be *unlike* in sound e.g. *right* and *fight* which is a **perfect** or **complete rhyme** with two identically pronounced consonants (*t*) two identically pronounced vowels (*i*), a difference in the previous consonant (*r* and *f*), and two identical stress patterns. *Right* and *fight* are **one-syllable** or **single rhymes** but there are also **double** and **triple rhymes** as in the two or three syllable *making* and *baking* or *slenderly* and *tenderly*. One syllable rhymes are sometimes known as **masculine rhyme** and two syllable rhymes as **feminine rhyme**. Some rhymes may now appear incorrect simply because the pronunciation of words has changed over the years – *love/move, wind/mind* are common examples of what is sometimes known as **eye rhyme**. A writer may sometimes choose to soften the effect of rhyme by using **half rhyme** or **para rhyme** in which the consonant or the vowel is different. Wilfred Owen's poems 'Exposure' and 'Strange Meeting' make frequent use of this device, with half rhymes of words such as *brambles/rumbles, years/yours, spoiled/spilled*. Another common device is **internal rhyme** where a rhyme is used in the middle as well as at the end of a line as in

> **And pillows bright where tears may light**

rhyme scheme   The conventional way of noting the pattern of rhymed line endings in a stanza or a group of lines. The letter *a* is used for the first rhymed sounds, *b* for the second and so on. Thus we can say that the rhyme scheme of 'Sir Patrick Spens' (p. 19) is *abcb*. The poem 'Hunter Trials' (p. 115) is *abab*; and the rhymes for the passages from 'The Canterbury Tales' are in couplets *aa, bb, cc*, etc.

rhythm, stress, metre   Rhythms and metres in English poetry are based on stress – the emphasis which we give certain syllables in *spoken* English. The pattern of groups of stressed and unstressed syllables in poetry together make up its rhythm. Thus when we say *Monday* the first syllable *Mon* is stressed and the second *day* is weak, whereas when we say *amuse* this pattern is reversed. The classic approach is to suggest that we can indicate patterns if we mark the weak and strong stresses in a line by using / to indicate a strong stress and x to indicate a weak one. In the line

> x   /   x   /   x / x   /   x   /
> **A book of verses underneath the bough**

we can see that there are ten syllables to the line which fall into five pairs, each with an unstressed syllable followed by a stressed one. This unstressed/stressed pair is very common in English verse and is known as an **iambic foot**. Where, as here, there are five such iambic feet in a line, it is called an **iambic pentameter** (*penta*- simply meaning *five* as, for example, in *pentagon*). Other lines containing different numbers of feet (from one to eight) are monometer (1), dimeter (2), trimeter (3), tetrameter (4), hexameter (6), heptameter (7) and octameter (8).

After the iambic foot, the trochaic foot (stressed followed by unstressed: /x is probably the most common in English verse.

> /   x   /   x   /   x   / x
> **Home art gone and ta'en thy wages**

There are several other patterns of syllables that according to classic tradition make up other different feet in English poetry such as the dactylic foot (stressed followed by two unstressed: /xx) and the spondaic foot (two stressed syllables: //) but we suggest that if you wish to pursue the matter further you should look to a specialist book such as *How Poetry Works* by Philip Davies Roberts (Penguin, 1986). You will find that in practice, stress patterns in English poetry are subtle and varied and that rhythms are rarely banged out in the mechanical manner that is perhaps suggested by applying classical rules of Latin scansion. It is more helpful for you to be able to hear and enjoy the dancing rhythm in this line

> **Love again, song again, nest again, young again**

than to know that it could be said to consist of four dactylic feet.

run-on line(s)/enjambement   Run-on lines of verse occur where the structure and meaning carry the reader's eye and ear directly over to the next line without a break. Enjambement reinforces this effect by ensuring that the second line has a weak rather than a strong opening syllable so that any break is even less noticeable.

simile   (pronounced *simmily*: note the plural is **similes** pronounced *simmilies*). A comparison between two things introduced by the words *like* or *as*. (See the notes on **metaphor** and **imagery** above and also Part A Unit 2 of this book pp. 6–10).

sonnet   A poem of fourteen lines, each line being typically an iambic pentameter of ten syllables. The two main types are the **English** or **Shakespearean sonnet**, consisting of twelve lines made up of three quatrains (*abab, cdcd, efef*) plus a concluding couplet (*gg*) and the **Italian** or **Petrarchan sonnet** consisting of an octave and a concluding sestet. The octave is eight lines in two quatrains rhyming *abba, abba*: the sestet is composed of six lines rhyming *cdc, dcd*; or *cde, cde*; or *cd, cd, cd*. The **Miltonic** sonnet is based on the Petrarchan form but there is no pause between the octave and the sestet – which generally rhymes *cd, cd, cd*. For examples, see *New Touchstones 14–16*, pp. 30–34.

stanza   Another word for a verse in poetry. A stanza has at least three lines, more often four, and is usually rhymed in a pattern which is repeated throughout the poem.

stress   All English speech has set rhythms of stressed and weak syllables. There is an agreed way of saying *Eng-lish* with an emphasis – or stress – on the first syllable *Eng-*; similarly the word *syllable* has a stress on its own first syllable.

syllable   Words may be broken down into their constituent syllables – the small speech sounds that go to make them up. Thus *bro-ken* has two syllables; *down* has only one; *un-der-neath* has three... and so on. A syllable must include a central vowel and may be preceded by as many as three and followed by up to four consonant sounds. The way in which words are split into syllables in English is fairly arbitrary so don't worry too much about it; trust your ear rather than any mechanical principle. In a word with several syllables, one syllable receives the main stress though others may receive secondary stress and may be regarded as strong or weak according to what seems to suit the poem's metre.

syllabic verse   Verse in which the total number of syllables in each line is regular. In practice, the number of stresses per line, not the number of syllables is what most English readers notice.

symbol   Something regarded by most people as naturally typifying, representing or recalling something else because it has similar qualities or because it is generally associated with it. Thus white is a symbol of purity, the cross is a symbol of Christianity, the lion is a symbol of courage.

vowel   An open and prolonged speech-sound made by using the mouth as a resonator as air is exhaled. A vowel can be a syllable on its own as *a* for example. The letters representing vowels are a, e, i, o, u.

ACKNOWLEDGEMENTS

The editors and publishers wish to thank the following for permission to reproduce illustrations:

The authors and publishers wish to thank the following for permission to reproduce illustrations:

AKG Photo for 'The Wave' by Hokusai on p. 7, 'Winter' by Arcimboldo on p. 13, the portrait of Geoffrey Chaucer on p. 144, the picture of the Miller on p. 149 taken from the Ellesmere Manuscript and the picture of the Pardoner taken from the Ellesmere Manuscript on p. 158.

The British Museum for 'The Ark' by Heath Robinson on p. 79.

Mary Evans Picture Library for the illustrations by Gustav Doré of the 'Rime of the Ancient Mariner' on pp. 83, 85, 87, 89, 91 and 93, the picture of John Clare taken from the frontispiece to 'The Village Minstrel' on p. 161, 'Alfred Lord Tennyson' by W H Mote on p. 167, 'Emily Dickinson' on p. 175 and the photograph of D H Lawrence on p. 182.

Life File / Nicola Sutton for 'Mother & Baby' on p.98.

The Bridgeman Art Library for 'Early Morning' by Samuel Palmer on p. 129, *Chaucer's Canterbury Pilgrims* by William Blake on p. 146 and the picture of the Wife of Bath taken from the Ellesmere Manuscript on p.149.

The Fotomas Index (UK) for 'The Gambler' by Holbein on p.154.

The Tate Gallery for 'The Lady of Shalott' by John William Waterhouse on p. 174.

Enitharmon Press for the photograph of Phoebe Hesketh on p. 188.

Topham Picturepoint for the photograph of R S Thomas on p. 193 and the photograph of U A Fanthorpe on p. 197.

"PA" News Photo Library for the photograph of Ted Hughes on p. 204.

The BBC for the photograph of John Agard on p. 210.

The editors and publishers wish to thank the following for permission to reproduce copyright material:

Anna Adams: 'Warning to a Worm', reprinted from *A Paper Ark* with permission from Peterloo Poets.

John Agard: 'Child Waiting', 'Limbo Dancer's Mantra', 'Rainbow' and 'Stereotype' reprinted from *Mangoes and Bullets* with permission from Serpent's Tail Ltd; 'Poetry Jump-up', 'Not-Enough-Pocket-Money-Blues', 'Smoke-loving Girl Blues', 'Spell to Banish a Pimple', 'A Date with Spring' and 'Half-caste' reprinted from *Get Back Pimple* with permission from Puffin Books Ltd.

Maya Angelou: 'Life Doesn't Frighten Me' reprinted from *And Still I Rise* with permission from Virago Press.

W H Auden: 'The Quarry' reprinted from *Collected Shorter Poems 1927–1957* with permission from Faber & Faber Ltd.

Basho: 'Crow' reprinted from *An Introduction to Haiku* by Harold G. Henderson. Copyright © 1958 by Harold G. Henderson. Used by permission of Doubleday, a division of Bantam Doubleday Dell Publishing Group, Inc.

James Berry: 'Workings of the Wind' reprinted from *I Like That Stuff*, Cambridge University Press, with permission from the author.

John Betjeman: 'Hunter Trials' reprinted from *Collected Poems* with permission from John Murray (Publishers) Ltd.

Edward Kamau Brathwaite: 'Limbo' and 'Cat' reprinted from *The Arrivants* with permission from Oxford University Press.

Alan Brownjohn: 'The Rabbit' reprinted from *The Railings*, Macmillan and Co Ltd, with permission from the author.

Buson: 'Parting' reprinted from *An Introduction to Haiku* by Harold G. Henderson. Copyright © 1958 by Harold G. Henderson. Used by permission of Doubleday, a division of Bantam Doubleday Dell Publishing Group, Inc.

Charles Causley: 'The Ballad of Charlotte Dymond' and 'What has Happened to Lulu?' reprinted from *Collected Poems* with permission from Macmillan and Co Ltd and David Higham Associates Ltd.

Richard Church: 'Quiet' reprinted from *The Collected Poems of Richard Church* with permission from Laurence Pollinger Ltd and the Estate of Richard Church.

Wendy Cope: 'Tich Miller' reprinted from *Making Cocoa for Kingsley Amis* with permission from Faber & Faber Ltd.

Frances Cornford: 'Childhood' reprinted from *Collected Poems* with permission from The Cresset Press.

John Cotton: 'Listen' copyright © John Cotton 1958 reprinted from *The Crystal Zoo – poems by John Cotton, L. J. Anderson and U. A. Fanthorpe* with permission from Oxford University Press.

E. E. Cummings: 'one', 'Hist whist' and 'in Just-spring' reprinted from *Complete Poems 1904–1962* by E. E. Cummings, edited by George J. Firmage, by permission of W. W. Norton & Co. Copyright © 1991 by the Trustees for the E. E. Cummings Trust and George James Firmage.

Paul Dehn: 'Alternative Endings to an Unwritten Ballad' and 'Exercise Book' reprinted from *Fern on the Rock* with kind permission of the Paul Dehn Estate, London Management Ltd.

Peter Dixon: 'Oh Bring Back Higher Standards' reprinted with permission from the author.

Carol Ann Duffy: 'In Mrs Tilscher's Class' reprinted from *The Other Country* by Carol Ann Duffy published by Anvil Press Poetry in 1990.

T S Eliot: 'Macavity: The Mystery Cat' reprinted from *Old Possum's Book of Practical Cats* with permission from Faber & Faber Ltd.

Max Endicoff: 'The Excavation' with permission of the author.

U A Fanthorpe: 'First Flight' and 'Travelling Man' reprinted from *A Watching Brief* with permission from Peterloo Poets; 'Casehistory: Alison (head injury)' reprinted from *Side Effects* with permission from Peterloo Poets; 'The Windsors: An Everyday Story of Royal Folk' and 'The Sheepdog' reprinted from *Voices Off* with permission from Peterloo Poets; 'Cat in the Manger' and 'Christmas Sounds' reprinted from *Safe As Houses* with permission from Peterloo Poets; 'BC:AD' reprinted from *Only Here for the Bier* with permission from Peterloo Poets.

Eleanor Farjeon: 'Cat!' reprinted from *Silver Sand and Snow* with permission of Michael Joseph Publishers and David Higham Associates; 'Cats' reprinted from *The Children's Bells* with permission of Oxford University Press and David Higham Associates.

Wilfrid Wilson Gibson: 'Flannan Isle' reprinted from *Collected Poems 1905–1925* with permission from Macmillan General Books.

Harry Graham: 'Appreciation' and 'The Stern Parent' reprinted from *Ruthless Rhymes for Heartless Homes* with permission from Edward Arnold (Publishers) Ltd.

Thomas Hardy: 'On a Pessimist' and 'Snow in the Suburbs' reprinted from *Collected Poems of Thomas Hardy* with permission from the Trustees of the Hardy Estate and Macmillan General Books.

Seamus Heaney: 'Blackberry Picking' reprinted from *Death of a Naturalist* with permission from Faber & Faber Ltd.

John Heath-Stubbs: 'The History of the Flood' reprinted from *Selected Poems* with permission from Carcanet and David Higham Associates.

Phoebe Hesketh: 'Clown', 'Sally', 'The First Day', 'Kingfisher', 'Owl' and 'Cats' reproduced by permission of Enitharmon Press from Phoebe Hesketh's *The Leave Train: New and Selected Poems* (1994); 'Fairy Story' and 'Remembrance Day' reproduced by permission of Enitharmon Press from Phoebe Hesketh's *A Box of Silver Birch* (1997).

Miroslav Holub: 'A Boy's Head' reprinted from *Miroslav Holub Penguin Selected Poems* (translated by I Milner and G Theiner) with permission from Penguin Books.

Ted Hughes: 'Wind', 'October Dawn' and 'The Jaguar' reprinted from *The Hawk in the Rain* with permission from Faber & Faber Ltd; 'Woodpecker' and 'Mooses' reprinted from *Under the North Star* with permission from Faber & Faber Ltd; '*From:* Spring Nature Notes' and 'Work and Play' reprinted from *Season Songs* with permission from Faber & Faber Ltd; 'The Warm and the Cold' reprinted from *Collected Poems* with permission from Faber & Faber Ltd; 'To Paint a Water Lily' and 'Snowdrop' reprinted from *Lupercal* with permission from Faber & Faber Ltd; 'Full Moon and Little Frieda' reprinted from *Wodwo* with permission from Faber & Faber Ltd.

Issa: 'In the House' reprinted from *An Introduction to Haiku* by Harold G. Henderson. Copyright © 1958 by Harold G. Henderson. Used by permission of Doubleday, a division of Bantam Doubleday Dell Publishing Group, Inc.

Richard Kell: 'Pigeon' reprinted from *Differences* by Richard Kell (Chatto & Windus) with permission from the author.

Kikaku: 'Full Moon' reprinted from *An Introduction to Haiku* by Harold G. Henderson. Copyright © 1958 by Harold G. Henderson. Used by permission of Doubleday, a division of Bantam Doubleday Dell Publishing Group, Inc.

Rudyard Kipling: 'The Way Through the Woods' reprinted from *Rewards and Fairies* with permission from A. P. Watt Ltd on behalf of the National Trust.

James Kirkup: 'The Bird-Fancier' reprinted from *Collected Shorter Poems*, University of Salzburg Press Vol 2: *Once and for all* (1996) with permission from James Kirkup and Oxford University Press.

Philip Larkin: 'Tops' and 'First Sight' reprinted from *Collected Poems* with permission from Faber & Faber Ltd.

D H Lawrence: 'Last Lesson of the Afternoon', 'Baby Running Barefoot', 'Bat', 'Wages', 'New Houses, New Clothes', 'Things Men Have Made' and 'Violets' reprinted from *The Complete Poems of D. H. Lawrence* with permission from Laurence Pollinger Limited and the Estate of Frieda Lawrence Ravagli.

Edward Lucie-Smith: 'The Lesson' reprinted from *A Tropical Childhood and Other Poems*. Copyright © 1961 Edward Lucie-Smith. Reproduced by permission of the author c/o Rogers, Coleridge & White Ltd, 20 Powis Mews, London W11 1JN.

Don Marquis: 'The Tom-cat' reprinted from *Poems and Portraits* by Sun Printing and Publishing Association. Reproduced with thanks to Bantam Doubleday Dell Publishing Group, Inc.

Roger McGough: 'Cup Final' reprinted from *Pie in the Sky* (Penguin Books) by permission of The Peters Fraser and Dunlop Group Limited on behalf of Roger McGough; 'The Commission', 'Out and About, the Lads' and 'The Railings' reprinted from *In the Glassroom* (Jonathan Cape) by permission of The Peters Fraser and Dunlop Group Limited on behalf of Roger McGough.

Spike Milligan: 'Soldier Freddy' reprinted from *A Dustbin Full of Milligan* with permission from Dennis Dobson, Publishers.

Edwin Morgan: 'Spacepoem 3: Off Course' and 'The Computer's First Christmas Card' reprinted from *Poems of Thirty Years* with permission from Carcanet Press Limited.

Gerda Mayer: 'May Poem' was first published in *Expression 7*, 1967, and subsequently in *The Candy-Floss Tree, poems by Norman Nicholson, Gerda Mayer and Frank Flynn* (Oxford University Press).

Grace Nichols: 'Snowflake' reprinted from *Give Yourself a Hug*, first published by A & C Black (Publishers) Ltd 1994. Published in Puffin Books 1996. Text copyright © Grace Nichols 1994.

Gareth Owen: 'Street Boy' and 'Unemployable' reprinted from *Salford Road* with permission from Collins Publishers.

Stef Pixner: 'Term Begins Again (Ostrich Blues)' reprinted from *Sawdust and White Spirit* with permission from Virago Press Ltd.

Po Chu-i: 'The Red Cockatoo' reprinted from *170 Chinese Poems* translated by Arthur Waley with permission from Constable Publishers.

Ezra Pound: 'In a Station of the Metro' reprinted from *Collected Shorter Poems* with permission from Faber & Faber Ltd.

Michael Rosen: 'Going Through the Old Photos' reprinted from *Quick Let's Get Out of Here* with permission from André Deutsch Ltd; 'When You're GROWN-UP' and 'You Tell Me' reprinted from *You Tell Me* with permission from Kestrel Books.

Ryota: 'Spring' reprinted from *An Introduction to Haiku* by Harold G. Henderson. Copyright © 1958 by Harold G. Henderson. Used by permission of Doubleday, a division of Bantam Doubleday Dell Publishing Group, Inc.

Shiki: 'Heat' reprinted from *An Introduction to Haiku* by Harold G. Henderson. Copyright © 1958 by Harold G. Henderson. Used by permission of Doubleday, a division of Bantam Doubleday Dell Publishing Group, Inc.

Sodo: 'Moon Magic' reprinted from *An Introduction to Haiku* by Harold G. Henderson. Copyright © 1958 by Harold G. Henderson. Used by permission of Doubleday, a division of Bantam Doubleday Dell Publishing Group, Inc.

Sora: 'The Barleyfield' reprinted from *An Introduction to Haiku* by Harold G. Henderson. Copyright © 1958 by Harold G. Henderson. Used by permission of Doubleday, a division of Bantam Doubleday Dell Publishing Group, Inc.

L A G Strong: 'Matthew Bird' reprinted from *The Body's Imperfection* by permission of The Peters Fraser and Dunlop Group Limited on behalf of L A G Strong.

May Swenson: 'Water Picture' reprinted from *To Mix With Time* copyright © May Swenson, first published in the *New Yorker*, with permission of Charles Scribner's Sons.

R S Thomas: 'Poetry for Supper', 'The Coming', 'Cynddylan on a Tractor', 'The Hill Farmer Speaks', 'Farm Child', 'Children's Song' and 'Welsh Landscape' from *Collected Poems 1945–1990* with permission from Weidenfeld and Nicolson.

Henry Treece: 'The Magic Wood' reproduced from *Black Seasons* with permission from John Johnson Ltd.

Kit Wright: 'Watch Your French' and 'Ghosts' reprinted from *Rabbiting On* with permission from Collins Publishers; 'The Song of the Whale' reprinted from *Hot Dog and Other Poems* with permission from Kestrel Books.

Andrew Young: 'Hard Frost' reprinted from *Collected Poems* with permission from Rupert Hart-Davies Ltd.